Seastone

American Indian Genesis

AMERICAN INDIAN GENESIS

THE STORY OF CREATION

PERCY BULLCHILD

Introduction by
Mary Crow Dog
AUTHOR OF *Lakota Woman*

Seastone

BERKELEY, CALIFORNIA

Published by: Seastone, an imprint of Ulysses Press
P.O. Box 3440
Berkeley, CA 94703-3440

Library of Congress Cataloging-in-Publication Data
Bullchild, Percy.
American Indian genesis : the story of creation /
Percy Bullchild ; introduction by Mary Crow Dog.
p. cm.
ISBN 1-56975-156-0 (cloth)
1. Siksika Indians--Folklore. 2. Siksika mythology. 3. Legends-
-Montana. 4. Creation--Mythology. I. Brave Bird, Mary II. Title.
E99.S54B83 1998
299'.72--dc21   98-30543
                                                                      CIP

ISBN: 1-56975-156-0

Printed in the U.S.A. by R.R. Donnelley

10 9 8 7 6 5 4 3 2 1

Editor: Steven Zah Schwartz
Production staff: Lily Chou
Design: Sarah Levin, Leslie Henriques

Distributed in the United States by Publishers Group West and in Canada by Raincoast Books.

837478

Contents

· · · · · ·

Spirit of the Sun

$\bullet \quad \bullet \quad \bullet \quad \bullet \quad \bullet \quad \bullet$

My name is Percy Bullchild, I'm sixty-seven years of age. I'm a Blackfeet Indian from Browning, Montana. We are of the former tribe of the Piegans. Others of this former tribe are in Canada—the Kainais of the Bloods, the North Piegans, and North Blackfeet tribe or band, all in Alberta, Canada. Our four tribes were once one big Tribe of the Piegans. We were split by the coming of the whiteman and their international boundary that presently divides the United States and Canada.

I do not have a good education of the whiteman language, I cannot speak it fluently. Unfortunately, I only went to the sixth grade and I couldn't speak English before going to school. And so the whiteman language is still very foreign to me. With what little education I have, I'm going to try to write the Indian version of our own true ways in our history and our legends.

Most written history of us Indians, the Natives of this North American continent, and the South American continent too, has been written by non-Indians. But this is our history and our legends of our beginning, the very beginning of all life. Most of these are so false and smearing that it gets me mad. That's the very reason why I'm writing now. We Indians do not have written history like our white friends. Ours is handed down from generation to generation orally. In this way we have preserved our Indian history and our legends of the beginning of life.

We don't tell of things that we hear from others, or recent happenings. Newcomers to Indian country did not teach us any of our history or how to tell a story. We do it ourselves. Things of the past are always in our minds, us old people.

My best informer of the past, both of history and the Indian legends, was my own paternal grandmother, Catches Last. She told me many things, many nights, when I was a very small boy. My grandma, Catches Last, passed away in 1927. Since her death, many others have told me of our historic past and our legends. Those that I still remember are Yellow Kidney, Weaseltail, Herman Dusty Bull, Two Guns White Calf, Jim White Calf, Many Hides, Bear Medicine, Shortman, Lazy Boy, Shoots First, Little Plume, Percy Creighton, Heavy Breast, Calf Tail, Little Leaf, Yellow Horn, and many others. All of these men that I have named have all gone on to our Happy Hunting Grounds, where all Indians go after death.

This story is about a lone spirit that lived in a spiritual place before there was a world or any kind of life. As he lived on and on, at one time it dawned on him that there was something amiss from this lonely life of his. There was an emptiness in his heart. Somehow! He must fill that empty feeling. This spirit was full of strange, mystic, and supernatural powers. He could do anything he wanted to do. He could transform into anything.

Death was nil to him, ever was his life. He has been alive from ever and will continue to live forever. Even to this day this supernatural and mystic being is still very much alive, and all of his mystic and supernatural powers are with us, among all of his creations of life. Life is given to all of us humans and to all of his creations on this earth and life is very abundant in Creator Sun's world today.

The sun came down and abided with his children in many instances to talk with them, to teach them certain things they must learn to use or do, and to give advice to them of how to survive the many treacherous things in this world he created for them.

Some of these stories may sound a little foolish, but they are very true. And they have much influence over all of the people of this world, even now as we all live.

BY MARY CROW DOG

* * * * * *

From the beginning of time there have been many legends among our different tribal peoples. Myths and legends of how this universe came about, how our people were created and how we fit into this life.

The story you are about to read has been passed on through the generations by the teaching of our elders. This particular story is from the Blackfoot Nation, but it shares much in common with stories of other nations: the birth from our creator the Great Spirit, how we relate with this universe, and how our elders pass on some of the wisdom as they know it.

Our stories bring forth the values we have always held—to respect our Mother Earth and all life; to remember the birth by which the Great Spirit brought forth life with earth, winds, fire and water; to take care of this Western Hemisphere as natural beings living in a natural order with all things.

Our stories remind us to care for all we have and be grateful for all that has been given to us. We learn to harvest and to replace what we gather by offering our sacred tobacco as thanksgiving to our creator and our earth mother.

From our elders we receive teachings for all generations, living and unborn, to carry on certain rituals—the living testimony of a natural people who have lived in harmony from the beginning of time. We carry on what our creator brought to us as man and woman knowing life, as women bearing life, as beings in tune with nature respecting our peoples.

We give prayers for the light, for the water we know to be sacred, for raindrops, for all the animals. In our stories, Mother Earth cries for Grandmother Moon. Our rituals bring a message of faith: the sacred medicine bundle is handed to our people so we can offer a prayer with sacred tobacco. We give the morning star prayer, offering cedar to bring the spiritual values of love of family and respect for our brothers and sisters. In this way we walk in beauty as a people.

Living in this modern society we must not forget our life cycle as we know it. We have been granted the gift of knowledge, the ability to use our sacred herbs and medicines, to heal with prayer. We must remember our relation to all beings and to the environment we live in. We must witness the taking of our earth mother and the polluting of the sacred elements that have been given to us by the Great Spirit.

Percy Bullchild's story is a message of peace for all peoples. We are living in a corrupted world. We have the choice of living our lives in a good way, the way of the Medicine Wheel—red, yellow, white and black united in the sacred hoop with the four winds.

We must be strong as a people to nurture our lives and honor our Mother Earth, for she is getting weak. We must save what we have so our unborn generations can uphold life. In caring for our soul we must remember the morning star, the light, the water of life, the air we breathe and the earth we walk on. We must bow down with respect to our creator or we may be faced with worse conditions—earthquakes, hurricanes, floods, tornadoes— our wake-up calls. We must stand up for the world we live in and we must remember the story of our beginnings, the story of life.

Earth's Beginning:
A True Story to the
Best of My Knowledge

* * * * * * *

Creator Sun has lived from the beginning and he will live on forever. He can do all the impossible and more. Creator Sun lived alone in a spiritual place for ages, no one else to be with, and naturally he got lonely for some kind of life to be with. One day he gathered the space dust and spit on it to make it into a clay. He had the future in his mind.

He could've shaped the mud into any form he wished, but thinking far ahead, made it into a round ball. Creator Sun blew into this mud ball. The blow gave the ball life. It became suspended in midair with air all around it to keep it in the air. There

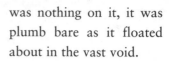

was nothing on it, it was plumb bare as it floated about in the vast void.

For the longest time he played with the ball as it floated about. He made himself small so he could play and romp on this ball of mud. For many eons of time, Creator Sun played and romped on this mud ball. But as time went along he got tired of it, he wasn't satisfied anymore. Again he began to think what else he should do to make things happier for himself.

"If only I can put something on it to make it look better," Creator Sun thought. Even then a plan was forming in his mind. Creator Sun thought of another life besides his. Another life would surely fill in that empty place in his heart.

From the dirt of this mud ball, Creator Sun again gathered dust, because the mud ball had dried up already. From this dust he made mud again, by spitting on the dust. And with the mud of clay he made a long, slim form. This was to become the first living being on this mud ball. It was a snake. Creator Sun made the snakes to multiply, to make their own, so they would become many.

For many eons of time the snakes flourished, increasing by manyfold. In fact, they had filled this mud ball and they were still coming. There were certain commands given them by Creator Sun to follow. As time went on, the snakes forgot all about the command of their Maker. They went wild. Everything they did went against their Maker. They weren't listening, they took everything in their own way. Creator Sun just couldn't stand any more of this, he had to do something fast. The snakes were coming too fast now, and he had to stop this in some way.

With his power, Creator Sun made this mud ball, the earth, boil out from beneath. This way, the snakes didn't have a chance to escape from this boiling dirt mixture. Creator Sun thought he got rid of all those snakes now. But, by a miracle, a very small female snake that was to have little ones escaped into a crevice— and for some reason, the boiling lava didn't ooze in this crevice. This small snake was saved, the rest were all boiled to destruction.

Some time after this destruction of the snakes, Creator Sun was walking around to see what had to be done to make up for this. As he walked along, he got a glimpse of the small female snake that was the only one to come out alive. Creator Sun only said, "From this small snake, let others come."

For the longest time again, there wasn't anything except the one snake that got away from all that boiling matter. Soon she had her little ones, and they were beginning to increase fast. Creator Sun, with his power, soon had them in control by using natural causes.

Creator Sun knew he was longing for something more than snakes, he just couldn't think of the right plan. One day, as he was playing and romping again in the dirt, he looked himself over. He was all dirty from the dust, and this got him to thinking about something else again—something soft to play on. It was then he invented the soft grass.

He made the grass so it would grow and grow, over and over. So the grass grew over and over—every time it got old and broken down, newer grass would grow in its place. Just like the snakes, it reproduced. All over the ball of dirt, the grass grew as cushion or carpet for the ground. It gave the ball of dirt color, too—a beautiful green carpet.

Creator Sun stood, admiring his work. It looked so pretty with the green now, and it was so soft to play on. But there was still something missing from this pretty ball of green. "I'll put pretty growth among the green, many pretty colors," Creator Sun thought. So the flower was invented to grow along with our green grass.

He sat down, and almost at the same time he sat down, a thought came to him, "I must make something in my own way— something that will look like my image." He was also thinking about the snakes and how they had reproduced manyfold. He thought, "I must make my image in a way so it will reproduce like the snakes."

Creator Sun finally knew what he was yearning for.

Moon and Big Dipper Come into Being

· · · · · ·

From the dirt again, from his dirt ball, Creator Sun made mud by spitting on it. From this mud he made a figure exactly like his image, only he made it to bear fruit—to have little ones. Creator Sun was very happy after the image came to life. He had blown in the nostrils of the mud figure, which gave it life.

This was the part he had been missing all this time. Creator Sun was very contented now. He knew he would have many new images from this mate he had just made. This new life started out just as he had wanted. His mate, the Moon, bore him a little one. This little one looked exactly like he did. It was a male.

Creator Sun became a teacher now. He taught the mate what she had to do in her job as a maker of their place. He taught the little one to help the both of them in whatever the work was. "This is the perfect way to live," Creator Sun thought to himself.

Things went smoothly for a long time. One day, Creator Sun noticed his mate was already big again and he knew they were going to have another little one. Time flies by, as all time does. It was no time before the second little one came to Creator Sun's family. The four of them lived very happy, because there wasn't anything dangerous to worry about.

Creator Sun's mate bore more little ones, between long intervals, until there were seven of them, the Big Dipper. The time went by. Each time he was trying to show one what to do, he would be uttering a certain sound. And as this utterance of a sound went along, it became understandable to each one—our language was started now.

Time lengthened into time. Their ways became routine for all of them. They would rest for a time and begin their tasks again. The boys grew bigger and bigger, and wiser, too.

As time went along that one snake, who had escaped the destruction of her kind, also had many little ones. With each new snake that came into life, the mother snake would relate her story of how the snakes were killed off by Creator Sun's doings—the boiling of the earth.

These little snakes didn't pay much attention to the story, except for one male snake, who had already grown up into manhood. This snake wanted a revenge for his mother's sake. At the time Creator Sun made the snakes, he had given them enough power to do certain things. Transforming themselves was one of those powers. With what little power the male snake had, he was going to do Creator Sun as much harm as he could.

Creator Sun's family was getting along so good. Each boy had a chore to do, their mother had hers—taking care of their living place and going after food for them in the thickets of nature. When all were at work, it was a routine thing for the woman to go off to herself to rustle what she needed for their camp.

It was one of these times the woman was alone. She was in a high growth of shrubs, looking for food. She got very startled by the appearance of another being. A tall, slim man, and in the same manner the boys and their father, Creator Sun, were made. At that particular time, handsome or good-looking wasn't heard of. But for some reason, the woman saw something extra special in this man's looks. She was completely overcome with surprise. She couldn't speak, she couldn't move, she just stood there and stared at this man.

For a long time they stood there staring at each other, probably waiting for each other to say the first word. It was a funny thing, they understood one another when they did talk. This was very unusual. It would seem that only nine of them would know their word. But the woman was just so startled, she didn't notice.

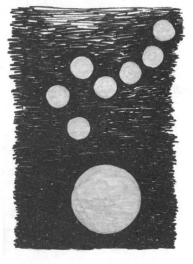

The Snakeman was the first to break the silence. "Don't be so startled. I'm a being just like you."

The woman was still startled and couldn't quite find words to say. Finally she said, "You scared me very much. I didn't know there were others the same as we are around this place. My husband, Creator Sun, never mentioned others to be around here."

"He must've forgot to tell you about us," the Snakeman told the woman. "But don't be afraid of me, I won't hurt you."

By now the surprise was gone from them, they both began to talk earnestly, eventually sitting down to visit. Both forgot time as they sat there visiting. All at once the woman jumped up, saying, "I'm supposed to be getting some things around here. I must hurry and get back, they will miss me if I do not get back to the camp."

The Snakeman jumped up too, saying, "I must be on my way, too. I have to get back to the others, before they miss me."

"Before you leave me," said the Snakeman to the woman, "I want to tell you not to mention our meeting here. If Creator

Sun has forgotten about us and never mentioned our presence here, then he must find out for himself that we are still around yet. Just keep this to yourself."

The woman readily agreed. She was a little nervous about it herself, too. The woman was a little late in getting home to her camp. There was no need to fear, though, no one was there yet.

Soon, each of the others began to come into camp for the meal and rest afterwards. For some reason, the woman felt quite uneasy. She really didn't have to worry, no one seen her with the strange man.

Creator Sun was always the last to come to the camp, he had quite a bit more to do than the rest of them. He came and sat down, he was quiet this time. For a long time he just sat there saying nothing. This made the woman that much more uneasy.

The woman too was unusually quiet, but she had to say something to break that awful silence. "What happened out there? Why is everyone so quiet? Maybe I can be of some help."

Creator Sun answered her, "Nothing happened. I was just wondering about a funny smell that's in the air. It's a wonder you and the boys don't smell it too."

Almost all at once, they answered, "We don't smell anything. It must be just a weed or something growing close by here, or maybe we went too close to some smelly weed." All got quiet again. The incident was soon forgotten and all began to talk of something else. Talking of something funny for laughter, to forget the smelly incident.

At this particular time, day and night wasn't separated yet. Everyone ate and laid down for rest. All slept for some time before waking up and then went back to the chores they had to do all the time. It was just a routine thing for them.

Several times the woman went out to where she usually gathered things for their use in camp. Each time she went, she had a secret hope of meeting the strange man she met there before. The Snakeman bided his time. He was always around when the woman was there, but in hiding so she wouldn't see him. He didn't want to spoil things for himself. The right time would come sooner of later.

One day the woman took her time getting out from camp. She always had other chores to do before leaving the camp area. Once through with the camp work, she got ready to leave for her own particular area. She had almost completely forgotten about the stranger she had met some time ago. Right at her busiest moment, she heard a noise behind her that made her jump with fright. Again she was startled by the sight of that strange man.

The Snakeman came again, and for some unknown reason the woman was thrilled to see him. She wasn't afraid to see him this time. Right away they sat among the growth and began to talk of things that happened since their last meeting here.

The woman mentioned that Creator Sun had some suspicion of their last meeting. Creator Sun said he smelled something peculiar. "We didn't know what it was, but I had a very good idea what it was. I never mentioned anything about our meeting. I was very near you the time we met, and I knew it had to come from you."

The Snakeman told the woman, "Just don't say anything about me yet, he will find out sooner or later. I like your company and I don't want to see it end so soon." The woman and the Snakeman both agreed to this. They would never mention this to anyone. It would be their secret for the time being.

The Power of the Snakeman

• • • • • •

Meeting the strange man was like a magnetic force to the woman. She was being pulled more and more to this Snakeman, but she didn't know he was originally of the once great Snake family that overran this land before her time.

The woman went more and more to the meeting place among the high growth of bushes. She made many excuses to cover up her wrongdoings. This thing was deep in her heart, an urge to see that strange man all the time. The strange man seemed to be there more often, and their meetings got more and more cozy. The meetings had become more cuddly. This went on for the longest time. Their secret meetings turned into very intimate doings.

After all the intimate meetings between them, the Snakeman knew it was a very secure friendship, and there was nothing to come in between them from here on. So he told the woman of his true identity. He told her about himself and the snakes' previous existence. That they were the first life on Mother Earth and were put here by Creator Sun. It was all snake life then, there were tiny snakes, medium snakes, big snakes, and great big, big snakes. He told her of the destruction of them and how one female snake got away by hiding in a deep crevice. She was in family way and not too far from having her little ones. She alone survived that great destruction of the inferno. All the rest of that snake life was destroyed.

He never mentioned why they were destroyed by Creator Sun. Naturally! The woman fell for the pitiful story. It was true to a certain extent, but the Snakeman made it so much more pitiful and worse. The woman felt awful sorry for that once great snake life and the way they were destroyed by Creator Sun. Maybe because of her feelings for this strange man, her feelings were now against her man, Creator Sun.

This woman of Creator Sun felt like she was the one to be responsible for what happened a long, long time ago. By doing what she was doing, the meetings with the Snakeman, she had the idea she was paying for Creator Sun's wrongdoings. She really didn't have anything to do with it at all, it was a long time before her time. This was the very thing the Snakeman was waiting for: to completely take the woman into his confidence.

He now had her where he wanted. She was on his side, it was very safe to tell her anything. He told her what to do if she wanted to get ahold of him. He took her to a very thick tangly brush not far from their meeting place. There, underneath the thick growth, where no one could see, was a den. Snakeman told the woman to just stomp over the mouth of the den as hard as she could with her foot, and that would bring him out from his den. It was this way for a long time, she would stomp over the mouth of the den and he would come out to meet her. It was her now that was bothering the Snakeman, and that's just the way the Snakeman wanted it.

Many, many times she knew she was doing very wrong, but that strong magnetic force kept her coming back over and over again. She knew she shouldn't be doing this to her man, Creator Sun, and to her seven sons. It was many times she made up her mind that she would not meet the strange man anymore. But she couldn't resist that strange force of attraction. Each time she left the Snakeman she wanted to go right back to him.

One of the times of rest, she finally noticed that her man, Creator Sun, hadn't said much in many days—in fact, for a very long time. He was just always so quiet now. She felt awful uneasy over this quietness. Creator Sun didn't come right out to accuse her, but that look in his eyes said enough for an accusation.

Creator Sun knew what was going on all this time, but, as always, he is so forgiving to all of his creations. He wanted her to overcome her wrongdoings by herself. This was his way of life. Creator Sun is never the mean type, because he made all things of this Mother Earth. He loves us all. But no matter who sinned against him or his rules, they will surely pay for the sin in their life, not after, because the sin was made in this life we are living here on Mother Earth. It really is our bodies that make a sin, not our spirits, and so the body has to go through some sort of payment for those sins we commit. It may be a sickness or it may be a broken part of your body, even death or whatever is a befitting way to pay for a sin, and it all comes the way it's set for the seriousness of the sin.

It was getting very close to where Creator Sun thought it should end, this wickedness of his woman. He knew of the Snakeman, because no one can hide anything from our Creator. Creator Sun left for his place of work, only this time he didn't go there. Creator Sun left, but went into the thickets to hide until his woman came out to her place of work. Creator Sun knew there was something going on. He knew it was her that the strange smell was coming from, he knew that no good was going on, but he must see it with his own eyes before he would believe it.

Creator Sun's woman was getting through with her camp chores and not hurrying much, she knew it wouldn't be too long before she would see her Snakeman friend. She got ready, and to the place of her work she went. She didn't even look to see if anyone was around, she went like nobody's business right to the den of her Snakeman friend. This time, there was her own man, Creator Sun, spying on her as he waited in the thick bushes. After she passed him, he followed her to wherever she was going, but followed so she wouldn't see him.

The woman went right for the very thick bushes after reaching her work area, and right on to the den of her Snakeman friend. Without a bit of hesitation she went to where she usually stomped to attract her Snakeman friend in the den. In a moment, a tall, slim man emerged from the thickets. He had a slim face, his body was very tall and slim too. This! Creator Sun was taking all in from his hiding place.

Creator Sun knew right away what it really was all about. He had recognized the strange man as one of those he had destroyed a long, long time ago. Creator Sun saw all that actually happened between the woman and her Snakeman friend. Creator Sun, after seeing what really happened between the two, hung his head in shame and sadness. His own woman was very bad. Creator Sun, sneaking away from there, went to his place of work. He went along sadly and in a deep thought about what took place. He knew what he must do, but it was work first at all times.

Day and night wasn't divided yet, it was bright out all the time. Each went to sleep for their rest except Creator Sun, he laid there thinking what should be done about his wife and her man friend, the Snake. After their rest, Creator Sun made sure the woman had gone to her usual place of work before getting into action. Instead of going to his place of work, he followed his sons to their places of work, each one of them. Creator Sun brought

all of the boys together in one place secretly, so the wife and mother of the boys wouldn't know of this meeting.

Creator Sun told his sons what was happening between their mother and her Snakeman friend. They were doing wicked things and something must be done about it. He consulted his sons so they could help him decide what to do. He told them all about the previous life of the Snakes. The Snakes had brought many evil things and wanted to run the land to their liking. Creator Sun told how he destroyed them by a natural disaster—not by his hands, but by his power of destruction.

"After what happened to those snakes, I really didn't think I'd have any trouble by them. I know they want revenge for what happened. That revenge seems to be working, they have your mother in their confidence and can do almost anything with her now. I must put a stop to this in some way before they ruin this land and before they try to get you boys too into their confidence.

"From now on into the never-ending time ahead I shall destroy the power I gave them, as much of it as I can. I shall make it so even you boys will despise those snakes or any snake that is seen. From here on, all people shall go against all snakes for evilness. People shall kill them anytime they see a snake."

The boys didn't care much about their mother after hearing about her and the Snakeman. What might become of her, they didn't care. They didn't want a mother like her. This was the very first experience about illicit behavior. To all of them it was the most wicked, the most evil thing that a woman could do, even if it was their own mother. All of the boys agreed with their father, Creator Sun, that the two should be punished—and for the rest of time—for their wrongdoings.

All came in for their rest and meal. The woman too came in a little earlier, for the first time since she had been meeting her Snakeman friend. After the meal all went to sleep as usual. The boys and their father, Creator Sun, were very quiet this time, no one saying much. This made the woman very nervous, she done this wrong and that, as she done her best to serve them their meals. She felt there was something awful wrong about all of this. Only the boys and their father, Creator Sun, knew they had condemned her.

Each of the boys got a special instruction for this coming period of work after their rest. Each knew what must be done in case of an emergency. All of them were ready as they all fell asleep. They woke up and all had their meal. No one seemed to want to eat, for some reason or another. The woman didn't eat much either. Getting up and leaving for their place of work, none of the boys went to their usual area. Instead, after getting out of sight from the camp, the seven boys met at a certain area preselected by their father, Creator Sun, and there they had to wait for whatever was going to happen next.

Creator Sun too left as the woman was busy with her chores. Creator Sun sneaked to the den of the woman's Snakeman friend. Before anything could go wrong—the woman just might accidentally hurry and get to her Snakeman friend's den—Creator Sun had to get there long before she might arrive.

Creator Sun wanted to get this over fast. He went directly to the very spot he had seen the woman stomping on. Creator Sun began stomping on the spot, and he didn't have long to wait. A commotion from within the den told him the snake was coming out. Creator Sun was ready with a big, large flint knife in his hand, poised, ready to strike.

This strange Snakeman would transform into a snake as he got ready to go into his den, and transform into a man as he came out all the way onto open ground. Just as the snake slithered to the open and his head emerged into sight, Creator Sun came down with all his might on the neck of the snake with the sharp flint knife.

The snake came slithering very fast to the surface, so when his head was chopped off, it fell to one side of the den. The snake's body kept a-coming until it was clear of the den before whipping around on the ground in its last throes of life. Creator Sun waited until the body of the snake laid still and in death before he ran for cover and to hide from the woman's view. Creator Sun had to wait to know what the woman was going to do about all of this.

It was a sad sight Creator Sun saw of the snake's death. As the head of the snake stopped rolling, there was a surprised look in his eyes, his tongue was still a-spitting out of his mouth. Towards the last of what life was left in it, the eyes became very sad and never stopped blinking until it laid still. Its eyes stayed open as it died.

Creator Sun's Revenge

• • • • • •

Hiding among the thick growth of bushes, Creator Sun waited for the woman.

The woman didn't wait too long, probably anxious to see her Snakeman friend. She left the camp area and went to her Snakeman friend's den.

Creator Sun was very quiet as he waited there. His ears were wide open for any kind of noise. The woman came a-stealing through the bushes when Creator Sun heard the rustle of her feet in the dry growth. Creator Sun almost melted to the ground hiding. Still, the woman almost brushed him as she went by. She must've been intent to get to the den, she didn't notice Creator Sun. Creator Sun, hiding there, felt very uneasy about all of this. He felt so lowly of himself, he felt ashamed, he felt guilty. After all, it was him that created these two that he was going to destroy. He already destroyed the whole snake population. He knew he should've done a good job of it the first time instead of letting that one female snake escape to bring in more trouble for him now.

The woman passed by Creator Sun's hiding place so close, he saw a smile on her face, a smile of happiness. He knew the smile wouldn't last once she saw what became of her Snakeman friend. In the next few steps she made, she came upon the remains of the Snakeman. The head was laying to one side and the body a little ways from the den. Her face turned to a horrified look as her eyes took in the whole situation. It was a pitiful sight to her. And the body, the head, looked so pained, he must've died an awful painful death.

The woman didn't know what to do. She froze in her tracks with fear and agony, slowly turning into rage and anger. For some reason, she knew it had to be Creator Sun that was to blame for this cruelty. For the longest moment she stood there gazing on her Snakeman friend, still as a statue, frozen with dismay. All at once she got her senses back, her voice again, she let out a scream, a bloodcurdling scream. For a few moments she took the head of her Snakeman friend and sat by the body, holding the two pieces together as if that would mend them together again. She was crying, sobbing, and screaming all the time. All at once she jumped to her feet, as if she remembered something very important. She began to run for the camp area. She ran with all her might as fast as she could go, and all the while she was screaming and crying at the top of her lungs. She was hysterical, like a maniac.

The boys were all waiting at the camp for their next move, and all had their instructions given to them by their father, Creator Sun. Hearing their mother screaming and the sound coming closer and closer, the boys began to make a roundabout way from the camp so their mother wouldn't see them. They knew they must get to their father, he had told them where the den of the Snakeman was at.

As soon as the woman made for the camp area and away from the dead Snakeman friend of hers, Creator Sun got busy. He jumped here and there, gathering wood and piling it close by the Snakeman, who was in his snake form now. He gathered a lot of wood already before the boys came a-running to the spot. They too began to bring dry wood to the pile their father already had. Creator Sun knew what the woman's next move would be, he made her from the dirt and should know her actions in every way. All of them were ready for the next move.

Finding the camp deserted, the woman didn't quite know what to do next. Without realizing what she was doing, she ran back towards where her Snakeman friend was slain. The boys and their father heard her awful screams, bloodcurdling, as loud as her lungs could sound. She was coming back to this place on a fast run.

As the woman was crying hysterically and screaming to the top of her lungs, at the same time she was calling her youngest son: "*Oo-ki-nah, Oo-ki-nah ki talk si-ni-tu, kahk sty in nah moo goo!* I'm going to kill you, no one will hold me from you!" If the woman could get ahold of all of them, she wouldn't spare any of their lives, including Creator Sun's life, if she could overcome his strange powers.

Her power was almost equal with that of Creator Sun. He had given her almost all of his powers. He never once figured this life would turn out like it was going now. He was so very sure of the perfect beings he was going to have on this land, and it was to be through her too.

The woman was so hysterical, she didn't notice the pile of dry wood not too far from her Snakeman friend's body. She came running into the area so fast too. She ran right straight for the body of that snake. She got on her knees and slowly laid on the snake body. As the woman laid across over her Snakeman friend's body, Creator Sun and his seven boys jumped out from the bushes they were hidden in and pounced on the woman. This was a complete surprise for the woman, she was overtaken by the whole ordeal. She didn't have time for any of her mysterious power that Creator Sun had given her to use for this purpose. Creator Sun and the boys didn't give her time for that. All this time she had thought they had left for places unknown.

With his big flint knife, Creator Sun stabbed her again and again until she laid still in death. His sons, all seven of them right alongside of him, helping him to do away with their wicked mother.

Creator Sun knew he had to make sure the two bodies were very dead, he must make sure there weren't any parts or bits of the bodies left. He must completely destroy every bit of those two bodies. Otherwise, with the mysterious power he had given them, they could come at him and his seven sons somehow.

He began to pile the dry wood, and on top of this he throwed the two bodies. He set the pile of wood on fire with his flint fire maker. The flames got bigger and bigger until the whole pile of wood was ablaze. Creator Sun had told his sons before this to watch very closely for flying sparks from the big blaze of fire. To be sure to throw the spark of ash back into the fire. Not to let even one tiny spark go, but to be sure it was thrown back into the fire. This was very important—that Creator Sun knew alone.

The boys took turns in gathering more wood for the fire to make very sure the two bodies burned to nothing, bones and all. The others, with their father, watched the fire very closely, almost non-stop, going around the fire watching for sparks. Each time a spark flew out of the fire, one of them would throw it back into the fire. All of them trying to see every spark that might come out of the fire, they all gave that attention as close as can be done.

Every once in a while, Creator Sun would prod around in the fire to test the bodies of the two, to see if they have burned to soft ashes yet. He would stir the fire thoroughly, the ashes, making sure the bodies were burning to nothing. He finally thought it was good enough, telling his sons, "Come on, let us go back to our camp now and do the best we can without your mother, she is gone now and we must carry on without her somehow."

Creator Sun was advising the boys that all must stay together for some time, just in case of an emergency. He told them he didn't feel all that safe yet about the two they done away with. "We should know by the time we have our fourth rest or sleep." It was a sad time at the camp, no mother to get the meals ready for them. They must take turns gathering food and preparing it—only the boys. Creator Sun had too much he had to take care of, so he was excluded from this work.

Creator Sun never hardly kept quiet. He talked away, giving his sons advice about what should be done in case something arises. "I will give each of you something to use in case of an emergency." To the youngest he gave a bladder of water and told him what he must do. To the next oldest son he gave a beautiful bird, he told him what to do if he called on him during such an emergency. Creator Sun gave his third-oldest son a bladder that was blown up with air, and told him what must be done with it. These bladders were made of roots and the leaves and barks of certain things, and made airtight by weaving them closely and tightly together. To his fourth son he gave a short stick to carry. To his fifth son Creator Sun gave a small rock to carry at all times until this state of emergency was called off, or until he would call on him for it. The sixth son got instructions to use his fingers. The oldest and the seventh son also got a bladder full of water, which he must carry until he should be called on.

All were sitting quietly, all sad over the recent events, waiting to see what would happen next. They heard a blood-chilling scream from the area of that fireplace. It made all of them jump to their feet.

This was what Creator Sun knew: if a spark came out of the fire, it could well mean a piece of the woman jumped out from the fire. Even a speck of her remains would bring her back to life and give her sons and her old man, Creator Sun, a bad time. Probably through her powers, a spark of her flew out of the fire undetected and here she is, screaming a bloodchilling sound. Her awful crying and those threats to all of them, especially to the youngest: "*Oo-ki-nah, Oo-ki-nah, ki talk si nitu, kawk sty in na moo goo!* I'll kill you, no one will hold me from you!"

From the camp they all left in a hurry, on a fast run. The youngest was put in the lead, and from there all of them strung behind him. Creator Sun was the last of them all. He took the rear guard for the sake of his boys. He loved all of them, even this woman that he put to death and who was now chasing them.

The woman, coming to the area of the camp, tracked the boys and her old man, Creator Sun. It made her much madder than she already was, they left before she could get her hands on them. She didn't realize the noise of her screams and the loud crying she was making. They would hear her coming in any direction.

It took no time for her to track them all, going from the camp on a run. All she had to do was to follow their tracks. This was one of the things that was overlooked by Creator Sun—to cover up their tracks. Anyway! Things were happening too fast for them now. It wasn't too very long before she was breathing down their necks. She was right in back of them. A few more steps, she could easily catch one of them—and that would be Creator Sun. He was running last. She tried to put on more speed, which took all the power left in her. She almost was stepping on Creator Sun's heels.

Creator Sun was hollering at the oldest son, "*I-stob-ska-spah-biks-it, ah-ni-yih, oi-ki-yi!* Throw the water bag up in the air towards her." As soon as the oldest boy heard his father calling for him, he didn't hesitate. The water bag went into the air. And as it got just above the woman, for a very mysterious reason, it began to rain on her. It was pouring rain. This slowed her down, the ground got soaked and wet. It made it slippery for her to run very fast.

It took a little time for the woman to realize she had power to use for this rain. She was just so very mixed up from this ordeal she was going through. Using that little power, the rain stopped, which put her on dry ground again. She picked up speed once on dry ground. Again she gained on those menfolks. Again those cries, the bloodcurdling scream, and those threats to all of her sons, even to Creator Sun. "*Kawk sty in nah moo goo wow, nook oose awk!* No one will hold me from you, my children. It's just too bad when I do catch ahold of you boys and Creator Sun."

Creator Sun hollered out to the next-oldest son, "*Hi you, hi you, nu koo yi!* My son! Just in the back of you, make a mark in the dirt with your finger, across our trail." The second-oldest boy done it just so fast. They were barely ahead of their mother. The mark in the dirt was made just a step or two before she got there. In a split moment, that finger mark became a canyon. The woman was caught on the other side of it. This mysterious canyon was very deep, with almost perpendicular walls on both sides of it.

At long last the woman made it across to the other side of that deep canyon. She didn't even take a breather after all the climbing. She went right back to her running and chasing the menfolks. In just a few moments more the woman caught up to them, and this time she was almost in reach of the oldest boy again.

It was time for Creator Sun to holler again, "*Noo-koo-yi, noo-koo-yi, hah-you, hah-you, awb-aht-dob-igs-it, ah-ni-yih, o-koo-took-yi!* My son, my son, throw back that rock!" The third of his sons threw the rock he was carrying back towards his mother. As that little rock hit the ground a mighty mountain range sprang up. As far as the eyes could see in either direction, north and south, there seemed no end to this mysteriously placed mountain range. There were sheer walls, deep canyons, rivers and creeks, and jagged rocks throughout. This jagged mountain terrain caught the woman again on the opposite side from the boys and their father, Creator Sun.

Running along the foothills, she came to a canyon into the rugged mountains. Into this canyon she made her way, going as far as the canyon went. From there she took her own route, she scaled those walls and jagged peaks. She went up, up, and up. At long last she finally made it to the top of them. Soon she was out in the open country. Away she went. If that climbing up and down those mountains made her tired, she didn't act it. Running this way and that way she soon found the trail of the menfolks. And from there she went as fast as her legs could carry her.

This time they were almost taken by surprise. Creator Sun hollered to his fourth son, "*Hah-you, noo-koo-yi, ni-tah-gaub-ot-obic-sit, ahn-ni-yi, miss-chis-yi!* My son, hurry, throw back that stick!" He didn't get through saying it when the fourth boy threw the stick in front of his mother. The stick touched the ground, when instantly! A very large forest sprang up.

After many, many tries, the woman finally got lucky and found a passage through this tangly growth of forest. The rage in her began to boil again. She tried her best to keep quiet as she steadily gained on them. Just behind them now, only a very little gap between them.

Creator Sun hollered to the fifth son: "*Hah-you, hah-you, noo-koo-yi, awb-aht-dob-igs-it, ah-ni-yih, koo-ma-paw-mah-ka-pi!* Throw it back, that you are running with!" No sooner said than done, the fifth boy threw an airtight bag of nothing but air in it. Of course, just before he threw it, he untied it. The bag landed right in front of their mother. As the bag hit the ground, a mighty wind came out of the bag. The forever mystery of Creator Sun's powers.

This wind that came from the bag was so strong and mighty, it carried the woman back where she came from.

She blew this way and that way, bouncing along by the force of this terrible wind when something stopped her. She had been blown against a tree, a strong one. She grabbed ahold before the wind could tear her from it. The wind blew and it blew, but she hung on. For the longest time she whipped around the tree. At last the strong wind abated and she was able to let go. Around in a circle she ran for some moments before coming onto a very faint track. She was back on their trail again, and now for a hot pursuit.

Creator Sun had to call on his sixth son, "*Hah-you, hah-you, noo-koo-yi, ishs-pobs-st-chis, ah-nah yi, sits-si-wy!* My son, throw the bird up in the air towards your mother!" Only halfway through his father's talk, the sixth son threw a beautiful bird into the air towards his mother. It was a many-colored bird. No sooner had the bird gone into the air when a very loud rumble was heard.

A streak of a light came from the rumble. Both the rumbling and the light seemed to come from a very dark cloud that formed instantly overhead. With this rumbling and the lightning, rain came also. The streak of light was hitting the ground just in front of the woman, and that rumbling noise was ear-splitting, it sounded so loud and sharp. And with it, water seemed to be pouring from above. This stopped the woman from going fast. She had to take her time, even stop at times to avoid getting hit by that streak of light coming from the dark clouds.

The woman didn't know what to make of all this, her first experience of thunder and lightning. The noise was so loud and sharp, she ducked around each time it thundered. And that lightning too, she had to duck from it or it would've struck her. But that little power she still had of Creator Sun's kept her from harm. Under a tree she waited and waited for this rain, the rumbling, and that powerful light that came out of those dark clouds.

The storm cleared up and it didn't take her too long to find their faint tracks, but they were a little hard to follow, the rain almost washed them away.

The boys were getting very tired from this running, it was so long ago that they were taking things easy around their peaceful camp. Something must be done about this running from their mother. They just couldn't run for ever from her. Something had to happen soon. Creator Sun's mind, too, was full. How to stop this nonsense? It shouldn't have to be like this. Creator Sun sensed something in back of him. Without any hesitation he hollered out to the youngest, "*Oo-ki-nah, Oo-ki-nah, hah-you, hah-you, ah-bah-da-soo-yin-it, ah-ni-yih, ow-ki-oh!* My son, my son! Spill that water back towards your mother!"

As the first drop of water hit the ground in front of the woman, she disappeared from sight. In front of her was an endless body of water, and the woman was caught on the other side. She started to scream again, cry again, those threatening rages. She was running back and forth along the shores of this great body of water.

This water spread so fast that Creator Sun, with his mystic powers, floated up into the air with the boys. They went up and up to get away from the water and the woman too. She was all alone now, running this way and that way to find a way across. She hadn't seen the boys and their father floating into the air yet.

The woman got smaller and smaller until she disappeared from their view. But that huge body of water even seemed bigger from up here, there just wasn't any end to it. The boys and Creator Sun drifted on ever upwards. As they drifted farther and farther away, knowing their mother was down there by the huge body of water, all of them began to beam with happiness. But that happiness was short-lived.

The woman sat there by the shore of the big, big water, thinking what she should do. The power she had left of Creator Sun— why not try to use it some way? The woman had a little of the sweet grass left. She took it and made a small fire. From this small fire she got some hot charcoals, and made incense from the sweet grass. She prayed as the sweet grass began to smoke, the smoke drifting upwards. By that mysterious power of the sweet grass smoke, as the woman stepped over it she became airborne. The mysterious smoke of the sweet grass lifted her up into the void. She found a way to overcome the water again and to keep on chasing those menfolks. For strange reasons that are unexplainable, the mysteries of our Creator Sun, the woman seemed to know which way those menfolks went or were drifting. She too went that way. She even found out she could go any way up there in the void. She could go fast or slow. It didn't take her long to find these things out. So again she began the chase.

Without any warning, the woman came up to them at a high speed. It almost cost one son's life. The woman used that mysterious power to her advantage wisely this time, but her power still wasn't any match with Creator Sun's powers. She made for the youngest, she came so suddenly. Just before she got ahold of him, Creator Sun threw his flint hatchet at her. The sharp blade of the hatchet got the woman right square on the left knee. It was with such force that the hatchet cut her leg off. She went down as her leg came off, and the boy was saved from his wicked mother once again.

This was a chance for Creator Sun to take back almost all of the powers he had given her. He ran back to her and stopped by her, as she cursed them all. He didn't mind the talking now, she couldn't do anything because of her severed leg. Creator Sun touched her on the top of her head with both of his hands and then ran the hands along both sides of her head and down both arms, as he talked mysteriously. All of this mysterious talk was the power of taking back those strange powers he had bestowed on the woman while they were together.

The woman wasn't giving up so easy, she was trying her best to jump up to Creator Sun as he stood by her. She still was full of fight, even with the pain of her severed leg. Creator Sun would touch her on the head every so often as he talked to her in a low tone. She just had to listen to the low-tone talk, no one can shut their ears from the mysterious powers of our Creator Sun. This still is true, even now as we live in this twentieth century. We all have to listen to him at one time or another.

Because of her threats to continue her chase, Creator Sun had to create a thing to rest by, as the steady chase was just too tiresome. It was then that day and night were separated. Half of the time the Moon would see freely, and the other half she would not be able to see at all. This was to hide Creator Sun and the boys in the darkness while they rested.

For four days the woman sat where her leg was severed by Creator Sun's hatchet. As Creator Sun was talking to her, she took her severed leg and held it to where it was cut from her body. She sat for four nights and days and her leg healed together by the mysterious powers again. But she didn't hold it just right as it was healing. It healed a little off, and now both legs looked like they were both the same side, both right legs.

Because of the blood she lost from her leg and the big sin she had done to Creator Sun, he told the woman, "All women from now on must shed blood to commemorate the beginning of night and day and to remember the unfaithful woman who lost her leg for her sin, and the blood of life that was lost by her."

If only Creator Sun had done away with all of those snakes he created for that first life to exist—if he hadn't thought of compassion for that lone female snake he let escape—he would've had a perfect life started here. Now he also put a curse on the snakes, that for the rest of time they must face death from all life. They would be stepped on and killed on sight by the human race, their wicked doings to our Creator Sun revenged. No rest for them either, like the boys and their father, Creator Sun.

For the rest of the Moon's punishment, she was left completely bare of clothing. No growth on her of any kind to cover her, and no bearing any offspring. So today, the astronauts find the moon completely bare, even of air or wind. It doesn't get hot from the sun's heat, just completely bare of any form of life. For

four days and nights, no one sees the moon before she becomes
visible again as a new moon.

Our Human Beginning

· · · · · ·

Our elders tell us, "This life we all have will come to
its end when Severed Leg the Moon catches Creator Sun and their seven sons, the Big Dipper."

This wasn't a happy ending, but a beginning for our kind of
life. The Moon was Creator Sun's very first creation, and then
his bride. For her wrongdoings to Creator Sun, she must be bar-
ren of all things, just as she is in these days—bare, but alive.

All of the attention now went to Mother Earth. From far
above, Creator Sun took care of his new wife. It was all spiritual contacts they made with one another to have many life forms
again, and power for Mother Earth to give suck and life to all
of their many children.

Today that spiritual power of both Creator Sun and Mother
Earth combined can easily be seen or felt: the warmness of the
rays of the sun, the many lives of this earth they have produced.
Plants, insects, fowls, animals—so many different forms of life,
we don't know all of them. Even the live elements for that life,
or for the death to them—lightning, thunder, wind, the many
kinds of storms. All of these bring life or death, as Creator Sun
wants it to happen. All of this became a routine way of life in

those very young and early days of the beginning of time, which was several billion years ago. But only yesterday for Creator Sun and Mother Earth.

Creator Sun came down to be with his new bride at times he had a chance to—when the Moon or Severed Leg was at rest for a four-day period and couldn't be seen. Each time he came down to be with her, he sensed something was amiss from their togetherness. He couldn't quite figure it out just yet.

She spoke of a little loneliness in her. She wanted company—life like her and Creator Sun. Before this, they had talked of more life for them on Mother Earth, but no certain kind. It didn't take long for Creator Sun to make his new woman happy. To the water's edge they went. From the mud Creator Sun molded a form in his own shape, his own image. The form completed, Creator Sun blew into its face and at the same time said, "Have the same kind of life we have and live to roam this land."

This mud figure came to life as Creator Sun blew into its nostrils. It got up from the ground where it laid and began to

walk. Its first try was very wobbly. Almost each try, he fell back down, but each time he got up he became stronger. It wasn't too long before this Mudman began to get around like his counterpart, Creator Sun. Like his mother, Mother Earth. His mind wasn't too good to begin with. But as he got better at things, in all, his mind improved too. As time went by, this Mudman got stronger and stronger. His mind was like that of his parents. It wasn't too very long before he done things just like his father and mother. He was a part of them.

As things got better for the new Mudman, Creator Sun took him out and began to teach him everything he knew of their own life and others. Creator Sun communicated with him in a way he could understand clearly. After a while of this, Creator Sun began to sense something wrong with the new son, Mudman. He wasn't so very happy with his time and the folks anymore.

On one of his visits with Mother Earth and Mudman, walking with the new son, Creator Sun heard him say, "If I only had someone like my mother to keep me company." This made Creator Sun realize the new son was very lonely. He needed someone to play with, especially the kind his mother was made like, opposite from him.

Creator Sun remembered well how he began to yearn for something before be made the first woman, Severed Leg. How good it was to have someone different than you. Someone to develop a seed of you. Mudman had grown gaunt from that loneliness. Creator Sun had to do something for him in a hurry. Up and around to care for all of that life, he went past the Mudman's bed. Mudman was fast asleep. This was the best time for that plan he had made in his mind. Creator Sun put the Mudman into a deeper sleep so he wouldn't know what was going on.

Kneeling down beside him, Creator Sun took out the Mudman's lowest, smallest left rib. With this rib he made an image after the Mudman and himself, and Mother Earth too. The form was like all of them, except it was made after Mother Earth. To bear fruit, to bear offspring. Laying the figure down, Creator Sun blew on the figure's face and gave it breath. As he blew on the face of this figure, formed after the three of them, Creator Sun spoke to it. "Now you have a life as we have and you are made after our son, the Mudman, to be his playmate. But you are made after your mother, Mother Earth, to bear others that will come from you and our Mudman son. You have breath like we have. The Mudman shall teach you what things you must learn to do. Most of all, be happy with your new mate or companion throughout time."

The Ribwoman too was very weak after she was created from the Mudman's rib. It took several tries and many days to be able to walk around by herself. Before the Mudman woke up, the Ribwoman was squirming around, wriggling and struggling to get up or sit up. She woke up the Mudman as she fell against him several times. The Mudman was so very startled to see another beside him as he woke up. At this time, the sex made no difference to him because he wasn't aware of the opposite sex just then.

Jumping up on his feet, the Mudman gave this new one water and some food to give it a start in its life. He helped her to down all of this, it made the new one much better afterwards.

From that time on, the Mudman became a steady servant to this newcomer.

As time went along, the newcomer got stronger and was able to do many of the things Mudman did. The two romped all through the fields, across the little running waters that were plenty all over. In short, they were having the time of their lives.

The two didn't have a stitch of clothing on to cover any parts of their bodies up. Neither of them was ashamed of the other. There wasn't any kind of sin between them, so they weren't aware of either's sex. Creator Sun wanted to familiarize his son, the Mudman, with the companion that was given to him, the Ribwoman. They had been together for a very long time now and must know what this life was all about.

As they were walking along and Creator Sun was thinking about future beings, the people, he turned to his Mudman son and spoke to him about that future all of them were going forward to. He told the son, "My son, you have someone to be with

you as you wanted, your wish as it is, the companion you have with you now is made after your mother, Mother Earth. She is made to reproduce whenever the time comes. Your woman is made to self-feed whatever she bears for you. This new companion of yours is made exactly like Mother Earth, to reproduce life—but it has to come from you, the seed that will be planted in her. In her, that seed will turn into an image of both of you. All of this you do not know yet. There will be a time when you will realize what I'm talking about and things will begin from there on."

Around that time the weather was somewhat like the normal days of this time. There were times when the air was cold at nighttime, even in the daytimes too. The two, Mudman and his Ribwoman, slept together to keep warm through the nights. It was one of these colder nights that it happened—what Creator Sun told his son, the Mudman. During this particular night, Mudman woke up late in the night from the cold. He felt as if he was freezing so he cuddled up to the Ribwoman to get warmed up. And in order to get warmth, the Mudman had to put his arm around the body of the Ribwoman. When his arms went around the body of the Ribwoman, and as he cuddled his body to hers, there was an extra warmth that emanated from the Ribwoman's body. This warmth from her caused him to have a funny feeling all over his body. The Ribwoman was fast asleep as he laid by her, keeping warm, and this funny feeling in him.

Having his arm around her body and with this funny feeling he had towards her, he must explore further what it was all about and why. So while the Ribwoman was fast asleep, Mudman explored the many parts of the woman's body. While doing this, something in him aroused from this hand exploration, especially when he touched the Ribwoman's private area. He had to find out further how different she was from him. His hands went all over her body, every inch of it. The Ribwoman woke up from all of this, the hands of Mudman feeling all parts of her body. She too got that feeling as she felt the hands of the Mudman going on all parts of her body. It was this time that they knew they weren't exactly the same as they had thought. What was being done now made their breathing much faster than usual. The Ribwoman just laid still as the Mudman's hands were feeling her body all over. For some strange reason, she felt ashamed, too ashamed to move or let the Mudman know she was aware of what was going on. Most probably, she must've liked it secretly. Anyway, it was something they found out about each other, the difference about them.

The Mudman came to realize what his father, Creator Sun, was talking about. For as they laid there, for those same strange reasons unexplainable to anyone, both him and her knew what else was to be done. Their first intimate relationship. This first sex act between them was very painful to the Ribwoman. But again, for strange reasons, she didn't seem to mind that pain very much, as she too had wanted to fulfill that yearning for one another that very night.

This was a true beginning of a man and a woman's true happiness and togetherness for the rest of their lives. At this time, it was to be a never-ending happiness and togetherness between the woman and the man. There wasn't anything to end one's life. No sickness to worry about, nothing to bring death. Life was forever. The two could now face anything that might come along, because their lives were like one.

Strange things happen. Before this sex act together, there wasn't anything to cover their bodies. The two were just completely naked. After their first sex act, it wasn't the same. For those strange reasons, they couldn't look at one another's private areas anymore, they had to cover theirselves up with something. It was then that getting the shameful feeling came into existence.

All the male life, especially the human life—and this went for the other too, the female life—they were to honor each other throughout their lives. All of the life was given to find a companion of the opposite sex and the one chosen was to last for the rest of our days. We were to bear more of the same as we lived along with one another. Our seeds were to be just for the two of us, the chosen mate. This was a sacred commandment by our Creator Sun.

Our father, Creator Sun, gave all of us a commandment to live by. He is the only Creator of all life, one maker. There isn't another like him to exist anywhere, no matter how many million lightyears, as the astronomer talks, away from this earth or wherever. There is no one like our Creator Sun. He alone gave us a commandment that was to be used by all, especially the human beings. The commandment was just a plain, "Be honest to life and to all life." This one commandment covered everything: Be honest.

We have all lost that one lone commandment by our Creator Sun that covered all of our wrongs. Our Indian life had one of the truest form of religion before the coming of the Europeans. We led a life according to our Creator Sun's commandment, which all of us were given to live by. The other nationalities broke that one great commandment. They broke away from it for the want of riches, greed for power, and to be notable. This is still a-going in these days yet. Lust for power, lust for riches, and lust for women. Every day we hear of this. No matter how high up in politics they might be, that lust for sin is always there.

Those European newcomers shamed us Indians into following that corrupt way of life and belief. In many cases, their way of faith is still somewhat confusing to the Indian because of their persecution of one another. We were led astray from our true religion and faith by these newcomers. We were brainwashed by those so-called missions that once flourished on all Indian reservations, and by those non-Indians that operated them. The Indian learned many bad things from these mission schools. We foresaked our true Creator Sun over the coming of the whiteman.

THE SEED OF
MUDMAN AND RIBWOMAN

• • • • • •

O ne day the Mudman and the Ribwoman were walking and romping out in those vast fields they had for a playground. Coming to a small creek, the Ribwoman told the Mudman, "Let's sit a while and rest. I'm just so very tired running and walking." Sitting down near the small creek, talking to one another in their happy ways and all about what they had done together so far. All at once the Ribwoman changed her talk, telling the Mudman, "I wonder what's wrong with me lately, I've been getting mighty tired and it seems that I'm carrying a heavy load for some reason."

Her words didn't surprise the Mudman. He knew from his father, Creator Sun, what there was to know about a man and woman's life together. How everything is planned out for the two of them. The little ones that the Ribwoman was to bear as time went along to make more of them in their likeness. The planting of a seed into the woman, how it was to take root in her and grow in her belly for a short time and then one day it would come out from her. This would become a creation of their very own. Creator Sun told him how long it should be before all of this took place, when the Ribwoman should expect the little image to come from her. This would be a little painful to her, but Mudman would be there to comfort her through all of this time.

The Mudman sat a little more closely by his woman, the Ribwoman, to comfort her. Putting his arms around her, he told her all about what was wrong with her, saying, "From now on you will have to take it easy. You must be careful of what you do. Leave those that might be too heavy. You mustn't run much anymore. You'll have to learn to do things slower and easier. In you, you have a little one that's like us. But we won't know who this new one will be like, you or me, until the new one comes out of you. Don't be scared, I'll help all I can to make things easy for you."

The Ribwoman was a little puzzled over all of this, she couldn't quite understand it all. She never had any experience of any of this. A little one in my belly and it will be in the likeness of either one of us, how come I'm carrying it in my belly, why isn't he carrying one too? These were some of the questions in her mind.

This little talk was soon forgotten. Life went on as usual for the two. There were some instances when she would feel movements in her stomach. Those movements in her got stronger as time went by, and it got that way both day and night now. It was a lot of waiting now, as he said it would be. Anxiety, pains both day and night, but Mudman would soothe her with his kind words all the time.

The Ribwoman got bigger and bigger as those days went on, and the movements got stronger each day. Each day came with a new experience to both of them, and the Mudman kept his woman on a move slowly each day and even at nights. Just like his father told him to do, she has to move all the time or that life in her will get too big and she would have a harder time to make it come out from her.

One night, late, the Ribwoman sat up moaning all of a sudden. Mudman woke up instantly, asking her what was wrong. He knew well enough what the wrong was, but he wanted to make sure. Asking her, "What's the matter with you, why are you moaning this way?"

"I'm having terrible pains in me. What's wrong with me?" The Mudman reassured her everything would be all right soon, not to worry too much. That little image of theirs would be coming soon and those pains would stop when it came.

All at once she let out a loud scream. She hollered to Mudman, "Help me, something is coming out of me, help me, help me!" Creator Sun had taught the Mudman all that he had to know about all of this. The Mudman didn't wait or get excited, he jumped to the woman's side, he threw all of his weight on the woman's belly and held her hands tightly. He told her to put her mouth against her shoulder and blow with all her might. She did what was asked of her. She wasn't making any more noise, she was just busy doing what she had to do. It was all over in a short while. The image of them came out of her. What a relief it was.

He knew what else was to be done, and that was to feed that little one from the mother's breasts. The new little one knew what must be done too. He went to work on his mother's breasts to fill himself with that fresh milk. This was the first born in this world, Mother Earth's body. This particular one was just like its father, the Mudman. He was a boy.

Things happened and things were coming into place. A pattern of what was to come now and in the future. As each piece fell into place and fitted into that pattern of life, those next things that were to come were much easier to absorb. One night as the three of them were in bed and ready to go to sleep, Ribwoman told Mudman, "I'm very sure that I'm on my way to have another of our own creations. But this time, I know we are ready for this one. We know just what to do when the time comes."

It didn't seem too long of a wait this time before the Ribwoman had another child. This second one came to them the exact image of the mother, Ribwoman. It was now a boy and girl, son and daughter, that the two had.

To the two, Mudman and Ribwoman, time was slow. But their family seemed to be running away on them. Their family was getting larger and larger. It had been a very long time since the birth of the first little one. There were several little ones now. Some were almost as tall as their parents, Mudman and Ribwoman. All were very happy, running and playing, as over those fields and hills they went.

These boys and girls of Mudman and Ribwoman grew older and bigger and their knowledge of life grew with them. They played on together, hiking, swimming, hunting for small things. Gathering wood and doing chores for their parents.

Mudman and Ribwoman taught them almost from their birth how to find food and what is food for them. The vegetation, the roots, the berries, and the different kinds of barks. How to preserve this food for later use. At this particular time of our beginning, there wasn't any kind of meat to use as food, so it was mostly vegetation that these first people ate.

While out doing these chores, the older boys and girls played sort of away from the smaller children, but kept their eyes on them. There wasn't any danger of any kind at this time, not even wild animals or anything that would harm them. Already these boys and girls, the older ones of Mudman and Ribwoman, knew all about adult life, without anyone teaching them. When out gathering food or doing chores such as gathering wood, these children would go an extra distance from their camp. These older brothers and sisters would play together as a man and woman, just like their father and mother lived. A boy would pair off with one of his own sisters and play man and wife, far away from their camp where no one would come stealing upon them. No one was the wiser when they came home. Their parents didn't know this, just as many parents don't know about their children in these days we are living. This man and wife play was always very close to a real life.

There were several of them by now that had grown almost into manhood and womanhood. These couples found a place behind bushes and in the deep grass to be their home. The boys would get together and play the part of getting food for their wives and their family. Things went along fairly well until they came to that part where it was played nighttime and time for a rest. Each of the pair went on behind those places they had picked for their home and where the others wouldn't see what was going on. There the man and wife play went on into the part of sleeping together. It was going fine for them all. But the very older ones had to make it so very real. They went all the way as a real man and wife, several of them. They knew it was not right for them to be doing this, which they found out some time after this.

So! Even in those very early days of Mudman and Rib-woman, in that young world, those very first children knew about sex and they knew it thoroughly. They had to play it among themselves, because then it was only them, all brothers and sisters that were brought into this world by their parents, Mudman and Ribwoman.

Some of the girls got pregnant by their own brothers and there wasn't anything the parents could do about this. Those girls were already getting big in their stomachs. From all of this makebelieve of being man and wife among those first brothers and sisters, a new life was in the making. Those boys and the girls, true brothers and sisters, same father and same mother, remained with their parents until their little ones came. After all those babies were born safely, then came a punishment for them all. Their parents had taught them of self-survival and so, in the trouble they were in, those boys were made to move away from their parent's camp with those sisters that had babies. Those boys had to provide for their sisters they got into trouble, and this was for the rest of their time. It really was this that helped spread human life a little more rapidly. Like our Creator Sun tells us, "All humans are related to one another, no matter what nationality you come from."

They were told by their parents, "From now on, you children that done wrong will have to move other places where there is more food to provide for you all. If you all stay together in a group, things will be a bit easier for all of you. All of you may come to visit at times whenever you want or when in need of advice from your mother or father."

Creator Sun's Gift of Food to His Children

· · · · · ·

The many groups of children of Mudman and his wife, the Ribwoman, left their parents in the four cardinal directions: east, south, west, and north. From there on those children scattered the world over. Those children of the first two people, Mudman and Ribwoman, are us, the many people of this world today.

The people increased by manyfold as each group intermarried. And as they increased in a particular group, that group broke up into smaller groups to begin another camp of people somewhere else. These groups left the others because if there were too many in one area the food they ate became scarce. For many, many years our only food was berries, the roots or leaves of the many edible plants, or the barks of certain shrubs and trees.

As Creator Sun visited Mother Earth one time, he saw his children mostly all out looking for something to eat. He had given them food to grow on and live on, and this food should be making them fill out on their bodies. Instead they seemed to all be getting thin.

Creator Sun went directly to their place of camps and there he was welcomed by all of the children. He visited with all of them as soon as he arrived. Afterwards, he singled out his son, Mudman, and took a walk with him out into the open fields. He had to talk with him. He said, "Son! These children of ours are coming so fast now, they are getting too numerous for the food I have given you to eat. I came for that reason especially. We will get you food that may be found most anyplace."

As the two got far away and out on the plains, Creator Sun stopped and both sat down beside a small running brook. Creator Sun took some of the mud again, as he had done when he made Mudman. And with his hands he molded a thing with four legs on it, a head and the body. The Mudman was astounded at his father's making. After this thing was shaped by Creator Sun's skilled hands, he made the thing's nostrils and held it up to his mouth. He blew very hard into this thing's nostrils. Creator Sun, as he blew into the thing, said to it, "Now breathe the air from me, my breath, and live with it like my children are now living with it. Eat the food of grass and foliage to fatten you and those in the same likeness as you. Abound in this land and become the food for my children."

It got up on its feet and was very wobbly as it tried to walk away from them. This new thing fell back down but kept on trying to stand up and walk. It became very exhausted from trying to stand and walk. It had to rest for awhile as it laid there. Creator Sun soon took advantage of this. He told his son, the Mudman, "We will have to make them so they too will become many, just as you children are. It won't take them long to bring out their images so there will always be enough around for food."

As this thing laid there from exhaustion, it fell asleep. While it slept Creator Sun took out of it a rib bone, and from this rib bone he made the female. Telling the Mudman, "This one shall be for the seed which will be planted in her by the first one I made and they will become many."

As the two new food things got on their feet and got steady, they began to graze around. They were eating the grass and the many kinds of foliage growing all over. Creator Sun told his son, the Mudman, "Now leave them be for a while. I will let you know when to start using them for your food." This particular creature of flesh became the animal known as the buffalo. The

true name that was given them by Creator Sun was *eye-i-in-nawhw*, or as it's translated, "shall be peeled." All the killed buffalo were peeled or as we know it, skinned, to get at the flesh for food.

All of the food animals—buffalo, elk, deer, bighorn sheep, mountain goat, rabbit, and all the others—were made and given to Mudman. He was given a lesson in how to stalk them, how to kill them, and how to dress all of them out. He was taught how to cook them and how to preserve them for later use. How to preserve the hides for use as clothing and shelter. The smaller animals were for clothing mostly and the larger ones for shelter, but all of them were for food. Mudman was taught not to waste any part of the animals, even the bones were used for something.

The food animals became many, much more than needed. In fact, too many now. Mudman had to call on his father, Creator Sun, once more for help to solve this. Creator Sun again molded the mud into more animals, a little different than those first food animals he made. He made these with sharp claws on their feet and sharp teeth in their mouths. He told these animals to go and help eat those animals with split feet, the food kind. And so in these days we see the mountain lions, cougars, lynx, the bear, the wolverine, and all other predatory animals.

While he was at it, to make very sure that the people would never run out of food, Creator Sun made the edible birds. He also made all the rest of the animals to mingle with the food kind. This was to kind of confuse the people, to keep them guessing what animals should be for their food.

"I must tell you, do not ever waste food when you get it. When getting it do not overkill the birds or the animals, kill just enough for all those with you to use. If you waste food, food will become scarce for you. It will be very hard to come by anymore."

These very words of Creator Sun, not to waste food, were handed and passed on to generation after generation, right up to my time here on Mother Earth. My father and mother told me those same words too, which we all live by, the older of us Natives. Of course, the younger generation pays no heed to all of this that our father Creator Sun had taught us, and so many of us go hungry. Today, we older Indians see this to be very true, especially among our own people and maybe the other nationalities too.

Beginning of Many Different Dialects

· · · · · ·

At the very beginning of the lives of Mudman and Ribwoman, when the few children born to Mudman and Ribwoman began this life we are in on Mother Earth, the words of their spoken language were very few. It was a real simple language. As the children of Mudman and Ribwoman scattered ever so far apart from one another, their languages changed more and more until none of them could understand the other. This happened to almost all of those small groups that had separated from one another.

Mudman and Ribwoman, being told by Creator Sun to go spread the good news of more variety of food, left the children they were living with at that particular time. Telling them they were going to seek their brothers and sisters that left a long time ago, to give them the good news.

Readying themselves the night before, the two left just before sunrise for their long journey. For many, many days they traveled before they came to the very first of their children's group. This group hadn't gone too far away yet, it still knew the spoken language. They told them of the food animals and fowls they were given to eat, and also more of the vegetation. Not abiding too long in one place, they went on to find more of their children.

For many, many more days they went on before coming to more of their children. As the two came within hearing distance of the camp, they heard the children talking. The language these children were using differed somewhat from the language they spoke.

It was in this time that the hand language first came into existence, to make their own children understand what they were talking about. With this newer language with the hands, the sign language, the two told their children about the food. In sign language, the talker spoke out audibly, and at the same time made signs with his hands of what was being said. For example, if the talk was about a bear, he would be talking about the bear and at the same time making like a bear, his fingers curled to his palms and hands held even with his chest, and then a sign of the bear's teeth in its mouth. If it was a bird of some sort, big or small, the sign of big or the sign of small would be used. And then the hands and fingers to the shoulders were flapped like wings for the bird sign.

It took the Mudman and his wife, Ribwoman, many, many moons to get the message of more food to all of their children. But nevertheless they covered the land as far as their children were scattered before returning to their own camp, and they were well satisfied with what they had done for all.

The First Sickness and Death

* * * * * *

Creator Sun was getting very lonesome for his wife, Mother Earth, and all of his children that were with Mother Earth. He wanted to pay them a good visit very soon. Always he had to wait until Severed Leg the Moon went into her four days of hiding. Creator Sun always took that advantage. As soon as she disappears, he comes down to Mother Earth and all of those that Mother Earth is taking care of. In no time he was by his son, the Mudman, and Ribwoman, telling them he didn't come for any certain reason, but that he was lonely for all of them and wanted a good visit with them.

Not long after his arrival there, he told the two, "Let's go for a long walk, we can visit as we go along." Walking and talking along leisurely. Talking about the beautiful place they had to live. Coming to a river, to its steep bank, somewhat like a cliff, the three of them sat down and hung their legs over the bank and looked down into the running water.

Just to do something while sitting there as they talked on and on, without noticing, they were picking small pebbles from the ground and throwing the pebbles into the river below. The pebbles hit the water with a small splash and then slowly sank down under. This they were doing, over and over, as they sat there visiting.

Ribwoman interrupted the friendly visit. Sitting up straight and with a very businesslike voice, she turned towards Creator Sun, saying as she turned, "Creator Sun, you are the most powerful being here, there isn't anything you couldn't do. No matter how impossible it may seem, you go ahead and do the impossible. You transform yourself into anything you want. You can make yourself small so you can hardly be seen or even not be seen. You can make yourself so large that you can be seen from anywhere. You can transform into an animal, a bird, a fish, a tree, or just anything you have in your mind. You're so highly intelligent, too, you control the wind, the weather, the days and nights. You are a very great supernatural being that controls all of this place, far up and down."

Ribwoman's turn of the leisurely conversation and visit made Creator Sun and Mudman sit up to listen to what she had to say. She continued, "Here we are, my man and I, we have come a long way to this present time. We have many, many children like you wanted us to have. Those children of ours and their children are having children too. Right down the line, children after children, and still many, many more to come.

"There are so many of us now that we are scattered out so very far and wide. We are so far apart that we do not meet our children anymore, we have lost contact with many of them. We have lost our language, too. Those first several groups that had moved away from us, they speak a far different language than the one we taught them all. We can't understand them anymore. The main thing is, we just don't worry too much about one another. We don't worry of those in the camp, and so on to all of our children's camps.

"My Father, Creator Sun! Isn't there some way you can make it so we can really worry about one another? There must be something that can be done with us that we might worry much about each other. Our lives, our bodies, ourselves." It took Creator Sun a very long, long time to find an answer for her. Creator Sun turned towards Ribwoman very slowly, as if he didn't want to answer the question, and was very much puzzled about the question.

Mudman was trying to cut in, saying, "We should let well enough alone. I'm satisfied with the way we are living now. Our Father, Creator Sun, knows what is best for us all." The two did not even pay any attention to what he was saying. They weren't even listening to him.

Creator Sun's answer to Ribwoman was, "All of you are my own children that I dearly love with all of my heart. I love all the things that I created for all of us. I love my wife Mother Earth and all that she beared for me. Ribwoman, my child! You do not understand what you are saying. What you just asked for is against all of my plans for all of you. You are asking about your life and your bodies and yourselves. If I affected your bodies in some way, it wouldn't be good for any of you and I really don't care to do anything like that. I made you all so that I would have something I could love very, very much for time to come. I don't want to do anything to your bodies just to make all of you aware of each other."

Ribwoman wanted it her way. She begged Creator Sun and nagged him to do her bidding. It was a long argument. But like always, the woman won. She was just too set on something that was bad for them all. She didn't take no for an answer. Creator Sun finally gave in to Ribwoman's asking, but not a total commitment. What Creator Sun told her was, "I'll make your bodies slow down with something that will make you feel bad for a few days, then the body will come back to normal again."

Ribwoman argued, "That's not even anything to worry about. We'll know that the body will be all right in a few days, it's no worry at all. Why couldn't you make our body lay still and never move again, so we can cry for those bodies that are that way? We can really worry then, we wouldn't know who the next one would be to lay still and never move anymore."

Creator Sun never was a one that argued with his children, although he knew best. So once more he gave into Ribwoman, but still not a full commitment. "All right, I shall give you your asking, but the body will only lie still for four days and nights and it will come back as it was before then."

Ribwoman argued on, "How could we be lonely for one another if they are to be as they are in four days and nights? It's no worry for any of us."

All three of them were still sitting on the bank and throwing those small pebbles down into the water. Creator Sun, seeing those little pebbles hitting the water with a little splash and then slowly sinking down to the bottom. This gave Creator Sun an idea as they still argued on, over how it was to be for them all.

He told Ribwoman, "You have talked me into it, you argued me into it. Still, I won't entirely commit myself to it. We will decide by a stone about the size of your fist. I will throw the stone into the water below, and if it floats on the water without sinking down under, my plan of everlasting life will stand. If it sinks, then we will go with your idea of life."

Knowing that rocks are heavy and would easily sink down under, Ribwoman knew she had won the argument, although the rock wasn't thrown yet. Ribwoman selected a good-sized rock and handed it to Creator Sun. Creator Sun held it for several moments. All at once, he threw it out to the middle of the river. The rock made a big splash. The three of them jumped up, their

eyes on the rock as it hit the water. The splash of the water set-
tled back to normal and to the uttermost amazement of Mudman
and Ribwoman—especially Ribwoman—that rock she had selected her own self floated downstream with the current. Down,
down the river it floated until it went out of their sight.

Creator Sun looked at the both of them with a smile on his
face and, speaking to them at the same time, said he was very
happy at that moment for what had happened to the rock, floating downstream. "There it is, both of you saw the rock floating
downstream with your own eyes. Now we all know how we are
to live our lives throughout our future, everlasting life."

Ribwoman wasn't at all satisfied with the outcome of this
argument, she still wanted it her way. She began arguing with
Creator Sun again. "This isn't a bit fair to me. We know that you
are a being that can control all things of life, all elements we have
on Mother Earth and even far out away from Mother Earth. This
really isn't any surprise to me that the rock floated away with
the current down the river. I'm the one that was to throw the rock
into the river. I'm the one that is arguing with you about my idea
of life here. We came from you, we should have some say about
our own lives, especially our own future to come. At least a little say."

Creator Sun was very surprised at what Ribwoman said, he
didn't care to have any further arguments with her. He was sad
about this, but he must let his children decide their own fate.
Creator Sun sadly told Ribwoman, "I shall have to let you have
your own way about your future. After all, it's yours to live.

You know what you really want for all of your children that were born from you. I love all of you, because you're really all mine. I made you all, created you all for me to love you all. I will not affect the rock you are to throw into the water with any of my powers, it is all up to you now and all of the children and for the rest of time to come."

Picking up a good-size rock, about the size of his fist, Creator Sun handed it to Ribwoman, speaking to her at the same time. "Now my daughter, this is your own choice. It is the fate for all of you now and for all to come in the future, for as long as life may go on in this land of Mother Earth."

Ribwoman threw the rock as hard as she could upstream. The rock flew high and far out in the middle of the river. The rock made a big splash as it hit the water, it made a skip or two, then down under the water it slowly sank. Ribwoman was very gleeful over this, this was a fair throw and she had her way at the same time.

It was a sad thing for Creator Sun. He alone knew what sadness was all about, he had gone through it before. Getting up from where he sat on the riverbank, with not very much to say anymore, he bid his children goodbye. His head was stooped over as he slowly walked away from his children, Mudman and Ribwoman. He was very, very sad about all of this happening.

People say that from this unhappy change in his plans for all of his creations, as he left his children, the Mudman and Ribwoman, he walked ever so slowly away from them with his shoulders and head stooped over, he was so sad from all of this. And as far as anyone knows, he's still stooped.

As Creator Sun slowly walked away, Mudman scolded his wife, Ribwoman. "I hope you are satisfied with your crazy askings. You have hurt our Father's feelings so much! He loved us all so very much, all of us and everything else he has put here with us. There is a time he will never come to us anymore to help us solve our problems. We should abide by his words. From here on, we will have to face your crazy idea of laying still, never to move our bodies any more for the rest of time. All of us, our children and all their children, have to face this. You have made a very foolish wish that has come true. I think you are selfish for what you have done."

Creator Sun hadn't gone too far yet. Mudman got up and chased his father, catching up with him. He tried to cheer him up. Mudman was talking about other things, trying to get that sad thought away from his father's mind. "When will you be able to come to visit us again, Father?" Creator Sun didn't cheer that easy. His mind was just too heavy at this moment as he kept on a-going. He hardly spoke to Mudman, but nodded his head silently several times.

Creator Sun finally broke his silence, and with a voice so serious and very decisive said, "I'm leaving you all, you children and the other lives that are here with Mother Earth. I'll be there with the others, your seven other brothers, the Big Dipper. I am not coming just for visits anymore. I'm not coming unless it's something very important that you children have to see me about personally. I want you all to call on me all the time. I will still hear all of you. My power is such as to hear the distant calls of help, and I shall always be ready to help everything I have created with Mother Earth."

One day one of their favorite young ones didn't seem as lively as it usually was. All that day that young one seemed to be more quiet and not able to move much, inactive. The child was complaining of feelings in his body. Towards evening, the child lay very still, just barely breathing. Late that night, things for the child seemed to get much worse. As the light began to show in the east, the little one had become very still. No more breathing, he laid limp. He was dead.

Both Ribwoman and Mudman jumped to him, picking him up and trying to make him breathe again. Taking him from one another and doing different things to bring him back to life, but to no avail. The two got very hysterical, running around inside of their tipi hollering, and Ribwoman screaming to the top of her lungs for someone to help them with the little one, to bring the child back to life.

All of a sudden, Mudman seemed to get his sense back to normal. The woman had the little child in her arms at that moment and was still running around, screaming wildly. Mudman was at the doorway just then, and as the woman ran past him, he grabbed her arm and pulled her towards him, stopped her.

She was still screaming for some help. Mudman had to holler at her to make her shut up so she would listen to him, to stop this foolish cry for help.

It took a long time for Ribwoman to quiet down to listen to Mudman. Mudman was talking soothingly to her. "You asked for this and now it's happened. Our Father, Creator Sun, told you and argued with you about the sadness this would cause us, including the children, all of life. Now we have our first one of the many heartaches and sadnesses you have asked for."

Mudman was now calling out to his father, Creator Sun, to come just once more and to help them with this new happening that had befallen them. He was begging for him, crying for him to come to their side once more.

Creator Sun felt very sorry for them, but things had already come to pass as it was wished. There wouldn't be another chance, and nothing could be done for that still body now. All Creator Sun could do at the moment was to comfort both of them and then have a good talk with them.

Creator Sun's voice was barely audible to the two as he began to speak. "Both of you have taken what happened very hard. Don't once think that just the two of you are the only ones hurt by all of this. My heart is hurt more than either one of you. I'm the one that made life, I created it for all things that are here on Mother Earth. To destroy any of them is not what I want for them. I wanted to see everything as it came to life and to leave it as it came throughout time.

"But now! That wish of yours shall have to be, my words can never be taken back and done over again. You wished it and it must stay as it is now throughout time to come. The only thing I can do now is to take the dead body of the little one back and return it to Mother Earth's body and leave the spirit of the body go as it wishes to. That spirit will live on. You will not see that spirit until you have gone to that same place it is now gone to. The body shall be as Mother Earth's body again. Mother Earth will take care of them that leaves their bodies with her, and their spirits go on.

"I want you two to wrap the body of the little one, our beloved child, in a tanned hide and bundle the hide and the body with a rawhide thong as tight as you possibly can. Take the bundled body into the woods and find a large tree with a large branch that protrudes to the east, and high enough so wild animals will not get at that body. On that branch, tie the body as secure as you can so it will stay there for years to come. The face upwards and facing the east. This will be the symbol of giving me back that body of the one that passed on. Together, I and Mother Earth shall take the still body back into the land of spirits. If ever you happen by this place where that body is tied to the branch, check it and you will see that we have taken the body back as we have promised. You won't find a body, but you might find nothing but dust then and a few bones."

After the tree burial Creator Sun again left the two, telling them, "You must be very careful from now on, there are many things that will make your bodies slow down and not feel good. Things that you might eat or drink will affect your bodies. Some of these things that are bad will eventually cause your bodies to lay still like this little child you have just put away. So from here on, take good care of yourselves and warn all of your children to do the same. Everyone that is alive. Spread the word to all and soon."

Mudman and Ribwoman eventually died after living for many, many hundreds of years, probably thousands of years. They left many children scattered out in these lands of North America and South America, and we are all still coming and a-going yet. It will be so until Creator Sun says otherwise. Today, we are faced with more troubles than that time. We have the nuclear power, many, many strange sicknesses, guns, knives, cars, airplanes, and wars. We face much more than just plain sickness, and we will be lucky if we survive the next hundred years. And that's the world over.

Medicine, Power to Heal and Prolong Life

· · · · · ·

it had been a long time now that sickness and death had prevailed among the children of Creator Sun and Mother Earth. Always looking down on them, Creator Sun took pity on them. They had enough punishment and they should be helped in some way.

Taking Mudman out into the countryside and into the woods, Creator Sun told Mudman to watch closely at what he had done. Out around the countryside, Creator Sun uprooted several kinds of plants. And as he pulled each one out, he named it and told Mudman what it was for, what sickness it would heal.

Now! There were more causes for that sickness and death. It wasn't disease this time, it was injury to one's body, such as cuts of the flesh, broken bones, eye injuries, cases of poison, the try at suicide, and so on. Once more Creator Sun saw that his children could use his help. It was very important to slow the death rate of his children so he decided to come to their aid once more.

"I must take you alone into the mountains, my son, and there I will teach you a way to overcome many of the deaths caused from those bodily injuries. We will have to go to a high hill"

As soon as they arrived there he took Mudman to the highest place, and there they both sat down. "Now, my son, I'll give you some of my power that can cure anything if you use it the way I teach you. Listen good, this is a song that goes with my power." Creator Sun sang a song and, being a song by a supernatural being like Creator Sun, Mudman didn't have any trouble learning the song. It stuck with him.

"Also, here is a feather that goes with the power. It is a feather of a redwinged woodpecker, for that particular bird is mine. It works for me. You shall use this red earth paint that I use all over my body, which is the same color of me at times too. The song, the feather of the red-winged woodpecker, and the red earth

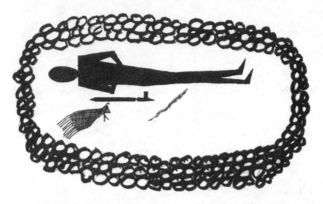

paint, along with a prayer to me, will help the sick or the injured get well, especially if you use the red earth paint to anoint their face. This is my power that you shall use for the good of the children.

"Furthermore, I shall give anyone powers if they seek it. To find the power is a little hard to do. First the one to seek power shall have to have a sweat bath to cleanse his or her body. One has to do this four consecutive days and nights, praying all the time.

"After the completion of this sweat bath, he then must leave the camps alone and go away out where no one else is around. No matter where you go, there is a power spirit there. Of course not all spirits are that all-powerful, but they are good for something. Spirits are up in the high hills, mountains, trees, rivers. All animals have supernatural spirits, the birds too. There is no shortage in the spirit world, but one shall have to seek them to find one. Once you get a spirit to like your way of reverence, it will come to you. From there on it will teach you what it expects of you and how you have to treat it. It may have some restrictions that one must follow to keep the spirit. Many spirits have such restrictions that they give along with the power. This is to keep the receiver of the power obedient to the spirit's wishes.

"When in seek of the spirit, one must pray at all times. One must have these things that are necessary to bring along on a seek for the spirit. It is a quest for a vision. The necessary things are a pipe, tobacco, your flint and striker, the dry moss, and, most of all, the incense. There are six different kinds: the cedar boughs, sweet grass, sweet pine, juniper boughs, sage, and the pine moss that hangs from the limbs of the pines. It looks like hair, either black or greenish gray. These you shall try.

"You are all alone, a way out from nowhere, no food for you to eat, because one has to be humble and act pitiful. You shall have no food for four days. If a spirit comes and gives you the power within the four days that are required, then food and water can be had. Remember! Only four days for one try, no food or water in those four days, just your smoking, your burning of the incense, and your prayers. If the vision is achieved within the four required days, then you could eat, but only after you have taken four more sweat baths to purify the body.

"Most often, a spirit will not bother you the very first night. Probably the spirit will be checking you over so the first night is usually an empty night. The second night is usually the time when the spirit will begin his test for your bravery. Away in the dead of the night, when everything else is still, a spirit will come to try and scare you away from your spot. A spirit will do anything to scare you—throw you around, drag you by your feet, pull your hair, anything short of killing. Maybe this will happen one night if luck is with you, but mostly this goes on for two nights or even right up to the fourth night. And if you stay with it and are not scared away from this spot, then the spirit shall give you his powers.

"A spirit shall put you into a trance or a deep sleep after you have proven your bravery. And while you are in this trance or deep sleep, the spirit will teach you what to do. And if there is a song that goes with the power, which there usually is, you shall learn every bit of what he has to offer you in power. It's funny how those powers work. After the trance or deep sleep, you will remember everything. Most all powers from the spirit world come with something that goes with the power—it might be a bone of some certain animal or bird, a certain kind of stick, maybe a rock, a feather, it might be a skin of some animal, a skin of some bird. Most all of the powers given by the spirits must have with it the earth paint of a special color. Also the pipe and tobacco comes with the power, these things you will have to get and keep on your person after you return from the vision quest.

"Everything you see around you on this Mother Earth—the growth, the air you breathe, the water you drink, the small stones, rocks, right to the big mountains, animals and birds, creatures of the waters, trees, bushes, just everything and anything of Mother Earth has a life and some of my powers to keep it alive. So there is no shortage of supernatural powers. Even within yourself this power exists. If you combine it with another source of power, it becomes supernatural. A human being can have several powers from the different spirits, and with the several powers, it would even be more powerful.

"All of the supernatural powers that are given are for the existence of our human life. The receiver of the power must use such power for the good of human life. They must help those that are afflicted by injury or sickness, anyone in need of medical help.

"Anyone that uses this strange power for the good of himself or for bad purposes, such as to destroy the life of another, to cheat someone or cause any type of harm to anyone, his or her bad wishes shall come back unto them and the power shall be taken away from them."

All of the existing lives of Mother Earth, Mother Nature— the dirt, grass, weeds, brush, trees, rivers, creeks, springs, brooks, and the great bodies of water, mountains, and so on—to me, these things of life are the ones that give power to people, every one.

Honoring
Creator Sun

· · · · · ·

Many, many hundreds of years went by. And all this time Mudman and his wife Ribwoman were alive and well, teaching their children what they had been taught by Creator Sun.

The two had many children, those children had many too, their children and their children having many more. As the population got too numerous, the people broke up into small groups and left for their own place to live. Now the population was so broad it must've spread out into most of the land, which today we know as the North American continent and South America too.

When Mudman and Ribwoman passed away, the people didn't have anyone to teach them what to do anymore, and all were taking things into their own way. Things were getting bad among the children of Mudman and Ribwoman, getting out of hand, no one around to correct them or teach them. The people went into a corrupt life, a bad life for most of them.

Creator Sun was always worrying about the life of his children, a good life he wanted them to lead. Creator Sun's mind was on the subject of how to make his children more aware of him and their lies, what was the best method for them to keep in their minds the reverence of each one's life and how to make them always thankful to him for that life he created for the purpose of compassion here on Mother. In other words, they had to know to thank him and Mother Earth always, because it is the two that is keeping them alive. The breath of Creator Sun and the suck we get from Mother Earth. Breath and food that comes from both of their elements, Creator Sun and Mother Earth.

One day as Creator Sun sat thinking of that matter, thinking of the smoking pipe and the tobacco he gave the first people to smoke and pray with as the smoke from the pipe slowly rose into the air and upwards, an idea struck him. "Why not use this method to keep their minds on the reverence I want them to keep in their minds."

Creator Sun knew that in some way women were very obedient to his ways if they wanted to be, but they could be just so hard to manage once they got out of hand. This was going to be a test in what he thought best for his children's ways, a way that would always remind them of his presence among them each day and night. He had a plan that would bring this holy way into the people without having to appear before them himself. At this time he picked out a very obedient girl, a teenager who still was a virgin.

Creator Sun had to hurry before this girl knew of adulthood. She was already thinking adult bad ways of life, but she actually hadn't done anything wrong. She had to be brought out of the wicked dangers of life. It was a summer night, and the day had been very hot. Many of the women were out gathering wood for their fireplaces in their tipis. It was late afternoon when they all left camp to go to the woods. None was in great big hurry, they were visiting as they gathered what was needed. It was

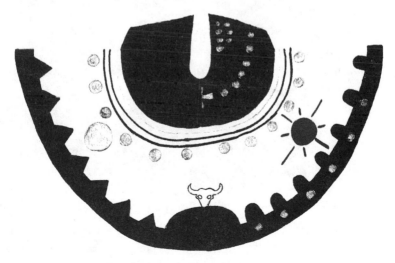

almost dark when all of the women started out for the tipis with the wood on their backs. All of them went along the trail without any trouble. This very nice girl that Creator Sun had in mind and her friend didn't go very far from where they gathered the wood, when the girl's load of wood came loose of the rawhide rope. She tied the load back together while her friend waited for her. On her back once more she threw it, and on their way they went.

They didn't get very far when the wood came apart again and fell to the ground again. The friend that was by her all this time was getting tired, the load on her back was getting heavy and she wanted to get it home to their tipi. This girl that was selected by Creator Sun didn't want to be alone, she talked her friend into waiting for her a little more.

She got her friend to take her load off and sit down beside her to rest for a while. The darkness had come and the night was moonlight, there were many beautiful stars shining bright from above. The two sat there among the trees, laying back and gazing up into the sky with its many, many stars. As the two laid there gazing upwards, the selected girl had her eyes on one particular bright star, a large one. It was shining so pretty, glittering in all sorts of colors.

She told her friend, "Look at that extra-bright pretty star shining in all kinds of pretty colors." Her friend agreed, she too was looking at this same star. Without waiting for her friend to say anything, the selected girl spoke out loud as she talked to no one in particular, "If that bright star was human, I would marry him, he is so handsome." Both of them giggled after she had said this out loud.

"Come on, let's get to our tipis, everyone else must've got their wood home and here we are still breaking down with our loads." They didn't get very far when the selected girl's load fell to the ground for the third time. "If your load falls again, I'm going to leave you. This load on my back is getting me very tired." Slowly tying her load together again, the selected girl got it on her back once more and off they went. They didn't go very many steps when her load came apart again. Her friend went on, telling the selected girl that the tipis weren't far, she could make it with her load after she tied it back together again.

She was getting tired from the load breaking apart and retying it so many times already, and she was slower to tie the load together this time. Kneeling beside her pile of wood, tying it together, her head bent over as she worked on the rawhide rope, when to her surprise a young man tapped her shoulder. As she turned to see who it was, the young man spoke with authority, "Come on, I came after you to come to my place. Come and let's put distance between here and get to where I want to take you!" The selected girl was taken aback. She had never been near men, she was a virgin yet. Why would a man come to get her? She didn't know any man.

She said, "I don't know you and don't know of any man or boy, so why should I go with you anyplace?"

The young man argued, "You said with your own mouth that you wanted to marry me."

The girl argued back, "No, no, I didn't tell anyone I'll marry him!"

The young man told the girl where she said it. "It was when you and the other girl, that went on to the tipis, when you and her were resting the second time your rope broke from your load of wood. You and her were laying back on your pile of wood resting, when you said, 'If that bright pretty star were a man, I'd marry him.' Well, I come after you, I'm that pretty bright star that shines with all of the pretty colors. Come on, we must get started before someone comes after you. You can't back down, it was your own wish." Taking her by her hand and arm, he pulled her up and led her away into the night. She couldn't back out from her wish, she had to go along with him.

It was still in the days of many mysteries. Her folks would miss her, but being left all alone in the forest, anything could happen to her. Wild animals could get her and eat her up, she could've lost her way, it was dark when the other girl left her. Many things could happen to her. Her folks and friends would look for her, but there would be no trace of her and they would all come to the conclusion that she must've been eaten by wild animals, probably a bear. No one would ever know it was a Star Being that took her away, and by her own wishes.

Through the trees the two went, the Star Being holding her hand as they went along. She knew it was no use to argue with this man. He was right, she did say that if the very pretty bright star were a human being, she would marry him. The girl didn't get scared as they went along for quite a ways. She was secretly tickled to know she was heard by a Star Being.

They had gone quite a ways from where this man had first appeared to her when he stopped. He told the girl to close her eyes until he told her to open them again. Without hesitation, she closed her eyes. She did not have to wait very long when he told her she could open them. She saw a very pretty valley with such nice fields and trees, but it was a strange feeling for her. She felt she didn't belong here. She didn't say anything to her new man, for she had a secret feeling of love for this Star Being. The Star Being told the girl, "This is your new place to live, here in this land we live. There isn't too many of us here yet, but we are increasing slowly."

After several days her parents became very, very bereaved, they knew something dreadful had happened to her. Many of their friends went out into the woods to look for her, but she wasn't there. In a very large radius from where her friend saw her last, they looked. They just couldn't find anything of her or her clothes, but they did find the pile of wood she left where the rawhide rope last broke from her back. After many days of looking, the parents gave her up for dead, killed by some wild animal and eaten. For a very long time afterwards, the parents mourned for their daughter, they loved her very much.

The girl got used to the new place, she came to love it because her man was from this land. She did whatever the other women were doing, her tipi chores first. She got to know all of their habits, their ways, the culture and traditional ways they lived. This selected girl got to love her Star Being husband very much. She had forgotten all about her own people and her parents. She lived with content among these people of her husband's. Always something new that she learned each day. She had been here for many years, she had grown up into an honest young woman, true to her husband in every way. She was an ideal lady.

Hole in the Sky

· · · · · ·

This day was another day in her husband's land, but it had come time again to dig for certain roots that were used for food. Roots were gathered at certain times of the year, mostly in the summer months or early spring of the year, when they are just fresh in growth. The women had to gather enough to last through the coming winter. This time it was the wild turnip roots that were to be dug and as always, this selected girl was very happy to go out into the fields. She had done this many times since she came here with her husband. The women made a regular party out of digging for roots. Lunches were made to take out and eaten after they were through digging for the day or sometimes about midday. It took several days for each kind of root to be dug out of the ground. Each one of the women would dig for so much or a bag full, then they were through for the day until the next morning when they went out again to dig some more.

The husband hesitated to let his wife go. For a long time, when the other women were getting ready to go on their first morning's diggings, the Starman argued with his wife about going out into the wild turnip fields. He had gone through the field with the other men, and all of these men had seen a special turnip out in the middle of a certain one of the many fields. A very large turnip, it must be four or five times bigger than the regular turnips, the leaves grew high and large. It could be seen as soon as one got into this field.

This Starman, having such powers to know what things were about, knew this was a year that wasn't going to be very good for him. He had dreamt about this long before now. His wife, the selected girl, argued back with her husband. She'd been out there digging with the other women ever since he brought her here. She told her husband it would be very lonely for her to be all alone here at the camps. There wouldn't be one lady or girl to visit with for the next few days, all of the womenfolk with their children would be out there digging for as many roots as they could get for the coming year.

After a long argument between the two, the husband finally gave in to her when she went out into the fields of wild turnips. "You must work along by one of the old ladies I'm going to tell to watch over you, so you do not forget this restriction. There is a very large turnip in one of the fields. Do not touch that one large one, don't even go near it. Use your ears and hear me right. It is a forbidden one of those turnips in that field. It is especially you that must not go near it, let alone touch it or try to pull it out from the ground. Hear me, hear me, my wife, and stay away from that one large turnip."

"I will, I will stay away from the turnip you are telling me about. You can tell the old lady to watch me out there in the turnip field. I have never gone against your words at any time since we've been together. I'll take your word that it will bring bad luck for us if I pull it out of the ground. I promise to not even go near it."

Everything went smoothly the first day. The second day of digging, all of the women went on into the next field of turnips and immediately went to work. They hadn't worked too long before one of the older women said she was getting mighty hungry. She didn't have to say it again when all of them threw down their digging tools and in the same spot they all sat down to enjoy their lunch. Soon after she got through with her meal the selected girl asked her overseer the old lady if she could come to the bushes to let her digested food out in nature's way. The old lady, sitting so comfortable, told her she could go alone, but hurry back, as it was nearly time to get back to work, they had to dig for so much of those roots each day. She didn't argue with the old lady—she had to go, and soon she could hardly hold her. She ran to the bushes and in among them to hide from the other ladies' view, so she could let her water run out.

It didn't take her long to get through and on her way back to the other women. Not far out of the bushes, right along the way she took, was this very, very large, extra-large turnip. It had the biggest leaves on it and it was quite a bit higher than the rest of the field of turnips. Seeing it made her stop in her tracks. It was a surprise for her to come to the forbidden turnip her husband told her to stay away from. This extra-large turnip didn't in any way look any different than the rest of the regular turnips in this field, it was only very much larger than the rest of them. In some mysterious way, this extra-large turnip had aroused her curiosity. She hesitated by it several moments, but in her heart she remembered her promise to her husband not to try to bother the extra-large turnip if by chance she came upon it. And this she did, she came upon it by chance.

It was very hard for her to walk away from this turnip. There was something about it that kind of pulled her to it. This turnip had a strange force, and she couldn't get it out of her mind. She tried to work hard to get it out of her mind, but it was just no use. It was a long day for her and she barely dug enough to fill her bag up this day. The extra-large turnip was too strongly on her mind.

There was a strange reason why she alone must not dig it. Of course, the restriction to not bother it was for all of the women. But for some reason she felt this restriction was directed at her mostly. The more she thought about it, the more curious she was.

Early the next morning the women and their children all went out into the turnip fields. This morning the girl was a little slower than other mornings. She was just straggling along in the back of all the women—even her overseer, the old lady, was among those ahead of her. This was the third day of digging for the turnip roots. The girl barely made it through this day, her thoughts were heavy.

The digging had gone on around a patch of trees in this field. The forbidden turnip was around behind the other side of the trees where one couldn't see. It was almost their lunch break when the girl got an idea. She must wait for the lunch break. It wasn't very long until one of the old ladies said it was time to eat their lunch.

The girl could hardly wait, she sat right down and ate as fast as she could. This would give her more time to do what she wanted during her rest period. She didn't lose much time after she ate her lunch. She asked the old lady, her overseer, if she wanted to go and relieve herself of water before the other women started to work again. The old lady didn't want to at this time, maybe later on, she said. She told the girl she could go alone if she had to, but to hurry and get back to start the digging again. The girl didn't even wait for her to get through saying what she had to, she jumped up and away. She ran for the thick growth of trees.

It wasn't anything unusual for a woman to go alone into the woods to relieve herself and come back and work again, so no one even noticed her. She didn't stop in the trees, but went right on through them, still a-running, and right to the extra-large turnip that was left all alone in this last field the women picked over.

This extra-large turnip had really made her nervous in the past few days, she was thinking all sorts of things about it. She just had to go back there and see this extra-large turnip once more. It had a magnetic force, it seemed to be pulling her back to it, her mind and herself. She came to the extra-large turnip. Its extra-large leaves, sticking up even with her knees, were very large, wide, flat, and long. She walked around it a couple of times, looking at it. This time, her mind was on her work and her overseer, the old lady. She had to get back soon, before the old lady missed her. She got ahold of those extra-large leaves and pulled on them a little bit. They seemed to give somewhat, and this gave her more courage to pull faster and with all her might. The extra-large turnip came up slowly as she pulled. She didn't ease any at all, and she almost landed on her seat when the turnip suddenly came out of the ground very fast from her last, hard pull.

The extra-large turnip left a deep hole in the ground where it grew, but the girl was busy looking at the turnip as it laid on the ground beside her. Her mind was on hurrying back now that she had pulled the turnip out of the ground and nothing happened this far. Jumping up fast to get to running back to the rest of the women, her glance fell to the deep hole in the ground, the deep imprint of the extra-large turnip. Not thinking of anything certain, she jumped on over to this deep hole in the ground and looked in it. She almost fell over with the biggest surprise of her life. The extra-large turnip left a deep hole in the ground, it was so deep that a light came from the bottom of it. The girl got on her stomach and looked down into this deep hole where the turnip came from. Tears came to her eyes as she laid there looking down into the hole. Almost directly below her was her people's camp. She recognized many of the tipis, she saw people as small as tiny insects walking around down there. One thing certain, it was her people's camp. She got very lonesome now that she saw her people far below the place she was at.

Getting slowly up again, she started back towards the women. Her heart was very heavy and those tears kept coming out of her eyes. She must get her self-composure before she got back to them. She mustn't let them know where she's been. Drying her eyes and wiping them the best she could and fixing up a little, she hurried back to the digging area. Most of the women were up and some had already started digging. She didn't wait, but went on to digging too, keeping her head down as much as she could until there wasn't any sign of tears anymore. She must get up some sweat to hide the tearstains on her cheeks.

This was her fourth day of digging the turnip roots, and already she had found out about the extra-large turnip that grew in that one field. It brought very sad thoughts in her mind. Those days she was at home with her parents and all of her friends. Thinking back on all of these precious times before she was taken away from her camp by this Star Being brought tears back again and again. It even made the day go so fast that it was time to quit before she knew it. Trying not to think of this anymore, she tried to bring herself together before they reached home, so her husband wouldn't suspect anything of her.

She had come out of the feeling before she got to her tipi, and looked like herself again. Her husband wasn't at their tipi when she came in, he was out somewhere, which made it all the better for her. She went ahead to make the evening meal, keeping as busy as she could to forget the day, but it just wasn't that easy to forget about seeing her parents' camp far below them that day. This kept on stirring her mind as she tried to forget the whole thing. It was just no use. After preparing the evening meal, she sat quietly alone, waiting for her husband to come home and eat.

THE ANCIENT PIPE BUNDLE

· · · · · ·

he Starman husband of hers came in just before dark, there was still light enough to see and eat their evening meal. Both were very quiet as they sat there eating, which was very unusual for the two—other times they were always busy talking. After their meal was gone, the Starman husband cleared his throat and asked his wife why she was quiet. He didn't wait for an answer, he went on talking to her, telling her that he knew already why she was so quiet this evening, that she found out about the extra-large turnip out in that one field. She had seen her parents' camp and had recognized them and now she was very quiet because she was lonesome for her real home, her parents' and her friends' camps. He told her that she shouldn't have broken her promise about not bothering the extra-large turnip root. He told her that they would have to go on despite of what happened. Furthermore, he made her promise with her heart that she wouldn't go against her husband's words the next time. The Starman also punished his wife for being disobedient to him. He kept her home in their tipi for the next several days.

The Starman husband couldn't stand his wife's loneliness any longer, he hadn't let on that he knew what was taking place with his wife, pretending all was normal. Early on the morning of the fourth day of her loneliness, the Starman went to a very wise old man to consult him about his troubles. The old man listened carefully to the young man. The old man, after he heard all, told the young man that this was very wrong, he should have waited before doing this wrong to a girl that hadn't known anything about adulthood yet. In a way, it was good that the two had found out soon enough, before there was a little one involved. This young man must bring his wife back to where she was originally from. Before he brought her back, he must give her something that was very valuable to all of these people of this land, the Ancient Pipe Bundle, to ease their parting for the both of them. This pipe would also make up for all of his wrongdoings.

The Starman husband went home to his tipi with a heavy heart, but he must let the girl know that he knew all along what happened to her, that she was a very lonely girl and he must take her back to her parents and her friends. He went in slowly, not a word from him as he made his way to his place of sitting, on his bed. His wife immediately realized what it was all about, being so very quiet. Somehow she knew this was a lecture to her and also something else more important.

Their living would be very different now since she found out about the forbidden turnip, and her loneliness would get worse. He told her that he had consulted one of the wisest old men around to find out what should be done about this. This wise man had given him advice that he must follow, and that was to take her back to her people. She would never overcome this loneliness, as she had pulled the only power that kept her here, the extra-large turnip.

He further told her they must get her ready before she left here, she must go through the mystical powers of Creator Sun that he had given these people. Also, this same power of the great spirits must be given to her to take as a sacred gift to her and her people. He said, "This readying takes about four days, well into the night of the fourth day, so you will be leaving me for good on the very early morning of the fifth day. You will travel with the rising sun. But now we must get ready for the coming event, a transfer of this very holy bundle to you, the Ancient Pipe Bundle. There's many things we have to do, prepare food for all of those that are taking part in the transfer of the holy pipe. Anyone that asks for this pipe, to own it as a keeper, must pay for it with their most valuable possessions. But that's almost only once in a lifetime to own a sacred thing like it. To you, my wife, it will not cost you anything. I'm giving it as gift to you especially, and this will eventually go about among your people. This Ancient Pipe Bundle comes from a long ways back, it is a gift directly from Creator Sun to sanction our thoughts of him always so we would not do bad things. I done wrong in what I done to you, but this Ancient Pipe Bundle will make things right for us both in the eyes of Creator Sun."

The two hurried along as the day went slowly, getting ready for the next morning. Everything had to be so in the Starman's tipi, and all of the elders must be invited to attend this great transfer of this Ancient Pipe Bundle. Both were so very tired when everything was ready the last evening. There was no time for thinking, there wasn't anything to think of for the girl, because she already knew she was getting ready to go home to her people. The only thing on her mind was that the days were so very slow from one day to another, these last four days with her Starman husband. In a way she hated to leave this man, yet in a way she was very glad she would be seeing her parents, her friends, and her native land again.

Her Starman husband was the one that was getting mighty lonely already, even though she hadn't left yet. But it consoled him when he thought of the way he took her away from her home, suddenly! The two fell on their bed and fell asleep as they hit the bed, they were so very tired getting ready.

At the end of the four days, all of the participants in this holy ceremony of the pipe bundle transfer have gone home to sleep and rest. The wise old man just moves across the room of this tipi and lays down to sleep and rest. He has done most of the main work of teaching the girl all about the bundle these last four days and he feels it now, he is very tired.

The girl selected by Creator Sun and Mother Earth and her Starman husband go to bed too, together for the last night of their marriage. Early the next morning, before the sun came up, they must be at that hole in the ground where the mysterious extra-large turnip had grown. It was a night to remember always for both of them—their last night together, never again shall they see each other. This was a punishment to both of them for the sin they had committed the way they got together in the first place. No one shall get by the sharp eyes of Creator Sun and Mother

Earth, it was wrong for them to get together the way it worked out.

It was still very dark when the wise old man woke up the two from wonderful sleep and told them it was time for them to go to the turnip field to do the rest of what has to be done. The wise old man carried the Ancient Pipe Bundle on his back.

On their way finally, it was still dark, the wise old man walked ahead of the two, leading the way with the holy bundle on his back and carrying one of the longest rawhide ropes anyone had ever seen. This rawhide rope was freshly stripped, it was green, very raw. Some of it was carried by the Starman husband. This fresh stripped rawhide was very heavy, but it didn't feel heavy to the two carrying it, the wise old man and the Starman husband. This is the ways of our Creator Sun, a very heavy burden is light when he takes a hand in his own makings.

Just outside of the camp of her people, the southeast side of this huge camp, other clans had moved in with this clan for the coming religious celebration that took place annually here. Up to this time, smoking of a common pipe was used for praying, and the tobacco was picked from the prairies. It wasn't a routine way of reverence. This smoking the pipe and tobacco was done any time and any place, whenever the people felt up to it.

Her people had seen something coming down from out of the sky as she descended slowly. Most of the people of this camp had gathered, watching her as she came downwards. They hadn't known what she really was from way down here. As she came closer and closer, the people made it out to be a human form tied to the end of a rawhide rope. But what was that? Something on her back, it was quite large, probably a child, maybe she was deformed on her back. All kinds of guesses.

The people followed her as she slowly descended to the southeast side of this huge camp. The people guessed just about the very spot she would land. Sure enough, it was there that she came down. But the fresh stripped rawhide rope wasn't long enough to reach all the way to the ground, it was short by a few feet. If the people of those days knew the foot measurement, they would say, "Short by about twenty-five feet." It was short enough for her to fall fairly hard the rest of the way to the ground as the wise old man and her Starman husband dropped her the rest of the way. Again, it was meant to be that way as a remembrance of this particular descent by the girl, just as Creator Sun wanted it to happen. She wasn't even hurt in the fall.

All of the people ran to her as she tumbled on the ground, but before they could come near her, she stopped them all by warding them off with the sign language of the hands. The people understood right away, they all stopped a little ways from her and all around her as she slowly got up to her feet. She asked for her parents by their name. No one in this crowd seemed to know who this girl might be. She had changed so much since she was taken away from here. It happened that the parents were in this crowd too watching her descend from up there. She, too, didn't recognize her parents, they had grown much older now, and her disappearance was an awful shock to the mother and father. Everyone thought the worst of it, no one in this crowd ever thought she would be seen again. So no one knew her at this time.

Her parents, hearing their names called by this girl came towards her slowly, as if afraid of her. She asked the two, her mother and her father if it were really them she was talking to. The parents hadn't recognized her either. They said it was their names that she called. Being confirmed by them personally and her knowing this was really her folks, she told them who she was. But there was a restriction before they could touch her that must

be taken care of at this time. They must make four sweat huts in a row near the creek where the water was gotten by the camps, and she must sweat alone in the first two huts. Then, the last two huts, she must be joined by her mother and father and as many of the wise elders that could get in this sweat hut with them.

This was no sooner said by her than it was done by mostly all of the available help that was at hand. It didn't take those people very long to complete those four sweat huts. They were completed with their covers, and the fire that went with each of them, and also the rocks that were put on the fire to heat until all of them were red-hot.

The parents of the selected girl didn't know whether to believe her or not until she showed them things on her body that only her parents knew of. It was time for rejoicing. After all of these years the parents thought they would never know what became of their daughter, and now they were feasting their eyes on her and she was still alive, only grown older with wisdom. Many feasts in the honor of her were given all over this large encampment. People were calling from all over the camps, hollering out invitations for the girl and her parents and the elders of this camp, singing and praying by many of the people for the return of this girl and the way she returned. It was an astounding mystery for the whole camp to see her come from the skies with only a fresh stripped rawhide rope tied around her middle and shoulders. Also, the holy bundle that everyone seen tied on her back—who would argue with that? She was telling the truth.

The morning of the fifth day, the girl told her folks that she must go on through with what she was told to do by the wise old man and her Starman husband. She must show her people how to conduct a religious ceremony with the Ancient Pipe Bundle. Her folks must enlarge their tipi so it could hold many of the elders. They must set up a double lodge, two tipis together to make one big room. It was done as she wished it, with plenty of help and the preparing of food to go with it. This was only to be a one-day honoring of this Ancient Pipe Bundle, and also to show the people of hers how it's done.

· · · · · ·

Our Natives had much faith in this truest form of religion, because everything was of the very nature they lived in. And most of all, our holy beings can be seen with our naked eyes. Our Creator Sun created the earth and all living things, from the beginning to this life we are living, and still he is creating new things. It has the power to destroy life through the many different ways of its own—storms, tidal waves, earthquakes, and even the wars that are fought by the human beings. Not only humans are affected through his powers, but the many kinds of life, too— birds, animals, insects, reptiles, and the living things of nature, be it a spiritual life of the surrounding growth of trees, rocks, mountains, any kind of water, stream, lake, and the oceans. Just think of what you may see in the newspapers: avalanches, landslides, floods, forest fires, breaking of dams, and volcanoes. People just don't have to believe it, but these are caused by our Creator Sun to punish the lives of the people for a wrongdoing they have committed towards his children or his creations of nature.

We see all sorts of life wherever we look, everything in this world of ours is alive with its own spirit of life. Even Mother Earth is alive. She feeds all of us, we all are her suckling children. Things come out of her body, the ground, growing up towards our father Creator Sun with their arms held out to him as the growth slowly grows upward from the ground. Everything is purified by nature as it grows along. Water too is purified as it sifts through the rocks, gravel, and sand. So our faith in the things we see with our naked eyes as they do their work for humanity is the Native's way of life.

Percy Bullchild was a full-blooded Blackfeet Indian born on the reservation in Montana. A well-respected artist and musician during his lifetime, he traveled thousands of miles each year to attend and perform at intertribal gatherings. He spent eleven years compiling the myths of his people.

Mary Crow Dog, author of the Introduction, is co-author of the *New York Times* bestseller *Lakota Woman.* A member of the Lakota Sioux tribe, she lives in South Dakota.